HUGO

A FANTASIA ON MODERN THEMES

BY

ARNOLD BENNETT

PART I

THE SEALED ROOMS

HUGO

CHAPTER I

THE DOME

He wakened from a charming dream, in which the hat had played a conspicuous part.

'I shouldn't mind having that hat,' he murmured.

A darkness which no eye could penetrate surrounded him as he lay in bed. Absolute obscurity was essential to the repose of that singular brain, and he had perfected arrangements for supplying the deficiencies of Nature's night.

He touched a switch, and in front of him at a distance of thirty feet the ivory dial of a clock became momentarily visible under the soft yellow of a shaded electric globe. It was fifteen minutes past six. At the same moment a bell sounded the quarter in delicate tones, which fell on the ear as lightly as dew. In the upper gloom could be discerned the contours of a vast dome, decorated in turquoise-blue and gold.

He pressed a button near the switch. A portière rustled, and a young man approached his bed—a short, thin, pale, fair young man, active and deferential.

'My tea, Shawn. Draw the curtains and open the windows.'

'Yes, sir,' said Simon Shawn.

In an instant the room was brilliantly revealed as a great circular apartment, magnificently furnished, with twelve windows running round the circumference beneath the dome. The virginal zephyrs of a July morning wandered in. The sun, although fierce, slanted his rays through the six eastern windows, printing a new pattern on the Tripoli carpets. Between the windows were bookcases, full of precious and extraordinary volumes, and over the bookcases hung pictures of the Barbizon school. These books and these pictures were the elegant monument of hobbies which their owner had outlived. His present hobby happened to be music. A Steinway grand-piano was prominent in the chamber, and before the ebony instrument stood a mechanical pianoforte-player.

'I must have that hat.'

He paused reflectively, leaning on one elbow, as he made the tea which Simon Shawn had brought and left on the night-table. And again, at the third cup, he repeated to himself that he must possess the hat.

He had a passion for tea. His servants had received the strictest orders to supply him at early morn with materials sufficient only for two cups. Nevertheless, they were always a little generous, and, by cheating himself slightly in the first and the second cup, the votary could often, to his intense joy, conjure a third out of the pot.

After glancing through the newspaper which accompanied the tea, he jumped vivaciously out of bed, veiled the splendour of his pyjamas beneath a quilted toga, and disappeared into a dressing-room, whistling.

'Shawn!' he cried out from his bath, when he heard the rattle of the tea-tray.

'Yes, sir?'

'Play me the Chopin Fantasie, will you. I feel like it.'

'Certainly, sir,' said Simon, and paused. 'Which particular one do you desire me to render, sir?'

'There is only one, Shawn, for piano solo.'

'I beg pardon, sir.'

The gentle plashing of water mingled with the strains of one of the greatest of all musical compositions, as interpreted by Simon Shawn with the aid of an ingenious contrivance the patentees of which had spent twenty thousand pounds in advertising it.

'Very good, Shawn,' said Shawn's master, coming forward in his shirt-sleeves as the last echoes of a mighty chord expired under the dome. He meditatively stroked his graying beard while the pianist returned to the tea-tray.

'And, Shawn—'

'Yes, sir?'

'I want a hat.'

'A hat, sir?'

'A lady's hat.'

'Yes, sir.'

'Run down into Department 42, there's a good fellow, and see if you can find me a lady's hat of dark-blue straw, wide brim, trimmed chiefly with a garland of pinkish rosebuds.'

'A lady's hat of dark-blue straw, wide brim, trimmed chiefly with pinkish rosebuds, sir?'

'Precisely. Here, you're forgetting the token.'

He detached a gold medallion from his watch-chain, and handed it to Shawn, who departed with it and with the tea-tray.

Two minutes later, having climbed the staircase between the inner and outer domes, he stood, fully clad in a light-gray suit, on the highest platform of the immense building, whose occidental façade is the glory of Sloane Street and one of the marvels of the metropolis. Far above him a gigantic flag spread its dazzling folds to the sun and the breeze. On the white ground of the flag, in purple letters seven feet high, was traced the single word, 'HUGO.'

From his eyrie he could see half the West End of London. Sloane Street stretched north and south like a ruled line, and along that line two hurrying processions of black dots approached each other, and met and vanished below him; they constituted the first division of his army of three thousand five hundred employés.

He leaned over the balustrade, and sniffed the pure air with exultant, eager nostrils. He was forty-six. He did not feel forty-six, however. In common with every man of forty-six, and especially every bachelor of forty-six, he regarded forty-six as a mere meaningless number, as a futile and even misleading symbol of chronology. He felt that Time had made a mistake—that he was not really in the fifth decade, and that his true, practical working age was about thirty.

Moreover, he was in love, for the first time in his life. Like all men and all women, he had throughout the whole of his adult existence been ever secretly preoccupied with thoughts, hopes, aspirations, desires, concerning the other sex, but the fundamental inexperience of his heart was such that he imagined he was going to be happy because he had fallen in love.

'I'm glad I sent for that hat,' he said, smiling absently at the Great Wheel over a mile and a half of roofs.

The key to his character and his career lay in the fact that he invariably found sufficient courage to respond to his instincts, and that his instincts were romantic. They had led him in various ways, sometimes to grandiose and legitimate triumphs, sometimes to hidden shames which it is merciful to ignore. In the main, they had served him well. It was in obedience to an instinct that he had capped the nine stories of the Hugo building with a dome and had made his bed under the dome. It was in obedience to another instinct that he had sent for the hat.

'Very pretty, isn't it?' he observed to Shawn, when Simon handed him the insubstantial and gay object and restored the gold token. They were at a window in the circular room; the couch had magically melted away.

'I admire it, sir,' said Shawn, and withdrew.

'Dolt!' he cried out upon Shawn in his heart. '*You* didn't see her at work on it. As if *you* could appreciate her exquisite taste and the amazing skill of her blanched fingers! I alone can appreciate these things!'

He hung the hat on a Louis Quatorze screen, and blissfully gazed at it, her creation.

'But I must be careful,' he muttered—'I must be careful.'

A clerk entered with his personal letters. It was scarcely seven o'clock, but these fifteen or twenty envelopes had already been sorted from the three thousand missives that constituted his first post; he had his own arrangement with the Post-Office.

'So it's coming at last,' he said to himself, as he opened an envelope marked 'Private and Confidential' in red ink. The autograph note within was from Senior Polycarp, principal partner in Polycarps, the famous firm of company-promoting solicitors, and it heralded a personal visit from the august lawyer at 11.30 that day.

In the midst of dictating instructions to the clerk, Mr. Hugo stopped and rang for Shawn.

'Take that back,' he commanded, indicating the hat. 'I've done with it.'

'Yes, sir.'

The hat went.

'I may just as well be discreet,' his thought ran.

But her image, the image of the artist in hats, illumined more brightly than ever his soul.

CHAPTER II

THE ESTABLISHMENT

Seven years before, when, having unostentatiously acquired the necessary land, and an acre or two over, Hugo determined to rebuild his premises and to burst into full blossom, he visited America and Paris, and amongst other establishments inspected Wanamaker's, the Bon Marché, and the Magasins du Louvre. The result disappointed him. He had expected to pick up ideas, but he picked up nothing save the Bon Marché system of vouchers, by which a customer buying in several departments is spared the trouble of paying separately in each department. He came to the conclusion that the art of flinging money away in order that it may return tenfold was yet quite in its infancy. He said to himself, 'I will build a *shop*.'

Travelling home by an indirect route, he stopped at a busy English seaport, and saw a great town-hall majestically rising in the midst of a park. The beautiful building did not appeal to him in vain. At the gates of the park he encountered a youth, who was staring at the town-hall with a fixed and fascinated stare.

'A fine structure,' Hugo commented to the youth.

'*I* think so,' was the reply.

'Can you tell me who is the architect?' asked Hugo.

'I am,' said the youth. 'And let me beg of you not to make any remark on my juvenile appearance. I am sick of that.'

They lunched together, and Hugo learnt that the genius, after several years spent in designing the varnished interiors of public-houses, had suddenly come out first in an open competition for the town-hall; thenceforward he had thought in town-halls.

'I want a shop putting up,' said Hugo.

The youth showed no interest.

'And when I say a shop,' Hugo pursued, 'I mean a *shop*.'

'Oh, a *shop* you mean!' ejaculated the youth, faintly stirred. They both spoke in italics.

'A *real* shop. Sloane Street. A hundred and eighty thousand superficial feet. Cost a quarter of a million. The finest shop in the world!'

The youth started to his feet.

'I've never had any luck,' said he, gazing at Hugo. 'But I believe you really do understand what a shop ought to be.'

'I believe I do,' Hugo concurred. 'And I want one.'

'You shall have it!' said the youth.

And Hugo had it, though not for anything like the sum he had named.

The four frontages of his land exceeded in all a quarter of a mile. The frontage to Sloane Street alone was five hundred feet. It was this glorious stretch of expensive earth which inflamed the architect's imagination.

'But we must set back the façade twenty feet at least,' he said; and added, 'That will give you a good pavement.'

'Young man,' cried Hugo, 'do you know how much this land has stood me in a foot?'

'I neither know nor care,' answered the youth. 'All I say is, what's the use of putting up a decent building unless people can see it?'

Hugo yielded. He felt as though, having given the genius something to play with, he must not spoil the game. The game included twelve thousand pounds paid to budding sculptors for monumental groups of a symbolic tendency; it included forests of onyx pillars and pillars of Carrara marble; it included ceilings painted by artists who ought to have been R.A.'s, but were not; and it included a central court of vast dimensions and many fountains, whose sole purpose was to charm the eye and lure the feet of customers who wanted a rest from spending money. Whenever Hugo found the game over-exciting, he soothed himself by dwelling upon the wonderful plan which the artist had produced, of his extraordinary grasp of practical needs, and his masterly solution of the various complicated problems which continually presented themselves.

After the last bit of scaffolding was removed and the machine in full working order, Hugo beheld it, and said emphatically, 'This will do.'

All London stood amazed, but not at the austere beauty of the whole, for only a few connoisseurs could appreciate that. What amazed London was the fabulous richness, the absurd spaciousness, the extravagant perfection of every part of the immense organism.

You could stroll across twenty feet of private tessellated pavement, enter jewelled portals with the assistance of jewelled commissionaires, traverse furlong after furlong of vistas where nought but man was vile, sojourn by the way in the concert-hall, the reading-room, or the picture-gallery, smoke a cigarette in the court of fountains, write a letter in the lounge, and finally ask to be directed to the stationery department, where seated on a specially designed chair and surrounded by the most precious manifestations of applied art, you could select a threepenny box of J pens, and have it sent home in a pair-horse van.

The unobservant visitor wondered how Hugo made it pay. The observant visitor did not fail to note that there were more than a hundred cash-desks in the place, and that all the cashiers had the air of being overworked. Once the entire army of cashiers, driven to defensive action, had combined in order to demand from Hugo, not only higher pay, but an increase in their numbers. Hugo had immediately consented, expressing regret that their desperate plight had escaped his attention.

The registered telegraphic address of the establishment was 'Complete, London.'

This address indicated the ideal which Hugo had turned into a reality. His imperial palace was far more than a universal bazaar. He boasted that you could do everything there, except get into debt. (His dictionary was an expurgated edition, and did not contain the word 'credit.') Throughout life's fitful fever Hugo undertook to meet all your demands. Your mother could buy your layette from him, and your cradle, soothing-syrup, perambulator, and toys; she could hire your nurse at Hugo's. Your school-master could purchase canes there. Hugo sold the material for every known game; also sweets, cigarettes, penknives, walking-sticks, moustache-forcers, neckties, and trouser-stretchers. He shaved you, and kept the latest in scents and kit-bags. He was unsurpassed for fishing-rods, motor-cars, Swinburne's poems, button-holes, elaborate bouquets, fans, and photographs. His restaurant was full of discreet corners with tables for two under rose-shaded lights. He booked seats for theatres, trains, steamers, grand-stands, and the Empire. He dealt in all stocks and shares. He was a banker. He acted as agent for all insurance companies. He would insert advertisements in the agony column, or any other column, of any newspaper. If you wanted a flat, a house, a shooting-box, a castle, a yacht, or a salmon river, Hugo could sell, or Hugo could let, the very thing. He provided strong-rooms for your savings, and summer quarters for your wife's furs; conjurers to amuse your guests after dinner, and all the requisites for your daughter's wedding, from the cake and the silk petticoats to the Viennese band. His wine-cellars and his specific for the gout were alike famous; so also was his hair-dye.... And, lastly, when the riddle of existence had become too much for your curiosity, Hugo would sell you a pistol by means of which you could solve it. And he would bury you in a manner first-class, second-class, or third-class, according to your deserts.

And all these feats Hugo managed to organize within the compass of four floors, a basement, and a sub-basement. Above, were five floors of furnished and unfurnished flats. 'Will people of wealth consent to live over a shop?' he had asked himself in considering the possibilities of his palace, and he had replied, 'Yes, if the shop is large enough and the rents are high enough.' He was right. His flats were the most sumptuous and the most preposterously expensive in London; and they were never tenantless. One man paid two thousand a year for a furnished suite. But what a furnished suite! The flats had a separate and spectacular entrance on the eastern façade of the building, with a foyer that was always brilliantly lighted, and elevators that rose and sank without intermission day or night. And on the ninth floor was a special restaurant, with prices to match the rents, and a roof garden, where one of Hugo's orchestras played every fine summer evening, except Sundays. (The County Council, mistrusting this aerial combination of music and moonbeams, had granted its license only on the condition that customers should have one night in which to recover from the doubtful influences of the other six.) The restaurant and the roof-garden were a resort excessively fashionable during the season. The garden gave an excellent view of the dome, where Hugo lived. But few persons knew that he lived there; in some matters he was very secretive.

That very sultry morning Hugo brooded over the face of his establishment like a spirit doomed to perpetual motion. For more than two hours he threaded ceaselessly the long galleries where the usual daily crowds of customers, sales-people, shopwalkers, inspectors, sub-managers, managers, and private detectives of both sexes, moved with a strange and unaccustomed languor in a drowsy atmosphere which no system of ventilation could keep below 75° Fahrenheit. None but the chiefs of departments had the right to address him as he passed; such was the rule. He deviated into the counting-house, where two hundred typewriters made their music, and into the annexe containing the stables and coach-houses, where scores of vans and automobiles, and those elegant coupés gratuitously provided by Hugo for the use of important clients, were continually arriving and leaving. Then he returned to the purchasing multitudes, and plunged therein as into a sea. At intervals a customer, recognising him, would nudge a friend, and point eagerly.

'That's Hugo. See him, in the gray suit?'

'What? That chap?'

And they would both probably remark at lunch: 'I saw Hugo himself to-day at Hugo's.'

He took an oath in his secret heart that he would not go near Department 42, the only department which had the slightest interest for him. He knew that he could not be too discreet. And yet eventually, without knowing how or why, he perceived of a sudden that his legs carried him thither. He stopped, at a loss what to do, and then, by the direct interposition of kindly Fate, a manager spoke to him.... He gazed out of the corner of his eye. Yes, she was there. He could see her through a half-drawn portière in one of the trying-on rooms. She was sitting limp on a chair, overcome by the tropic warmth of Sloane Street, with her noble head thrown back, her fine eyes half shut, and her beautiful hands lying slackly on her black apron.

What an impeachment of civilization that a creature so fair and so divine should be forced to such a martyrdom! He desired ardently to run to her and to set her free for the day, for the whole summer, and on full wages. He wondered if he could trust the manager with instructions to alleviate her lot.... The next instant she sprang up, giving the indispensable smile of welcome to some customer who had evidently entered the trying-on room from the other side. The phenomenon distressed him. She disappeared from view behind the portière, and reappeared, but only for a moment, talking to a foppish old man with a white moustache. It was Senior Polycarp, the lawyer.

Hugo flushed, and, abandoning the manager in the middle of a sentence, fled to his central office. He had no confidence in his self-command.... Could this be jealousy? Was it possible that he, Hugo, should be so far gone? Nay!

But what was Polycarp, that old and desiccated widower, doing in the millinery department?

He said he must form some definite plan, and begin by giving her a private room.

CHAPTER III

HUGO EXPLAINS HIMSELF

'And what,' asked Hugo, smiling faintly at Mr. Senior Polycarp—'what is your client's idea of price?'

For half an hour they had been talking in the luxurious calm of Hugo's central office, which was like an island refuge in the middle of that tossing ocean of business. It overlooked the court of fountains from the second story, and the highest jet of water threw a few jewelled drops to the level of its windows.

Mr. Polycarp stroked his beautiful white moustache.

'We would give,' he said in his mincing, passionless voice, 'the cost price of premises, stock, and fixtures, and for goodwill seven times your net annual profits. In addition, we should be anxious to secure your services as managing director for ten years at five thousand a year, plus a percentage of profits.'

'Hum!'

'And, of course, if you wished part of the purchase-money in shares—'

'Have you formed any sort of estimate of my annual profits?' Hugo demanded.

'Yes—a sort of estimate.'

'You have looked carefully round, eh?'

'My clients have. I myself, too, a little. This morning, for example. Very healthy, Mr. Hugo.'

'What departments did you visit this morning? Each has its busy days.'

'Grocery, electrical, and—let me see—yes, furniture.'

'Not a good day for that—too hot! Anything else?'

'No,' said Mr. Polycarp.

'Ah!... Well, and what is your clients' estimate?'

'Naturally, I cannot pretend—'

'Listen, Mr. Polycarp,' said Hugo, interrupting: 'I will be open with you.'

The lawyer nodded, appreciatively benign. As usual, he kept his thoughts to himself, but he had the air of adding Hugo to the vast collection of human curiosities which he had made during a prolonged professional career.

'My net trading profits last year were £106,000. You are surprised?'

'Somewhat.'

'You expected a higher figure?'

'We did.'

'I knew it. And the figure might be higher if I chose. Only I do things in rather a royal way, you see. I pay my staff five hundred a week more than I need. And I allow myself to be cheated.' He laughed suddenly. 'Costume department, for instance. I send charming costumes out on approval, and fetch them back in two days. And the pretty girls who have taken off the tickets, and worn the garments, and carefully restored the tickets, and lied to my carmen—the pretty girls imagine they have deceived me. They have merely amused me. My detective reports are excellent reading. And, moreover, I like to think that I have helped a pretty girl to make the best of herself.'

'Immoral and unbusinesslike, Mr. Hugo.'

'Admitted. I have no doubt that if I put the screw on all round I could quite justifiably increase my profits by fifty per cent.'

'That shows what a splendid prospect a limited company would have.'

'Yes, doesn't it?' said Hugo joyously.

'But why are your clients so anxious to turn me into a limited company?'

'They see in your undertaking,' replied Polycarp, folding his thin hands, 'a legitimate opening for that joint-stock enterprise which has had such a beneficial effect on England's prosperity.'

'They would make a profit?'

'A reasonable profit. A small syndicate would be formed to buy from you, and that syndicate would sell to a public company. The usual thing.'

'And where do I come in?'

'Where do you come in, my dear Mr. Hugo? Everywhere! You would receive over a million in cash. You would have your salary and your percentage, and you would be relieved of all your present risks.'

'All my present risks?'

'You have risks, Mr. Hugo, because your business has increased so rapidly that your income is out of all proportion to your capital, which consists almost solely of buildings which you could not sell at anything like their cost price in open market, and of goodwill. Now, I ask you, what is goodwill? What *is* it? Under our scheme you would at once become a millionaire in actual fact.'

'Decidedly an inviting prospect,' said Hugo.

He walked about the room.

'Then I may take it that you are at any rate prepared to negotiate?' the lawyer ventured, staring at the fountain.

'Mr. Polycarp,' answered Hugo, 'I must first give you a little information and ask you a few questions.'

'Certainly.'

Hugo halted in front of Polycarp, close to him, and, lighting a cigar, gazed down at the frigid lawyer.

'Till the age of twenty-eight,' he began, 'I had no object in life. I was educated at Oxford. I narrowly escaped the legal profession. I had a near shave of the Church. I wasted years in aimless travel, waiting for destiny to turn up. I was conscious of no gift except a power for organizing. That gift I felt I had, and gradually I perceived that I would like to be the head of some large and complicated undertaking. I examined the latest developments of modern existence, and came to the conclusion that the direction of a thoroughly up-to-date stores would amuse me as well as anything. So I bought this concern—a flourishing little drapery and furnishing business it was then. I had exactly fifty thousand pounds—not a cent more. I paid twenty-five thousand for the business. It was too much, but when an idea takes me it takes me. I required a fine-sounding name, and I chose Hugo. It was an inspiration.'

'Then Hugo is not your—'

'It is not. My real name is Owen. But think of "Owen" on a flag, and then think of "Hugo" on a flag.'

'Exactly.'

'I began. And because I had everything to learn I lost money at first. I took lessons in my own shop, and the course cost me a hundred a week for some months. But in two years I had proved that my theory of myself was correct. In ten I had made nearly a quarter of a million. Everyone knows the history of my growth.'

Polycarp nodded.

'In the eleventh year I determined to emerge from the chrysalis. I dreamed a dream of my second incarnation as universal tradesman. And the fabric of my dream, Mr. Polycarp, you behold around you.' He waved the cigar. 'It is the most colossal thing of its kind ever known.'

Polycarp nodded again.

'Some people regard it as extravagant. It is. It is meant to be. Hugo's store is only my fun, my device for amusing myself. We have glorious times here, I and my ten managers—my Council of Ten. They know me; I know them. They are well paid; they are artists. A trade spirit must, of course, actuate a trade concern; but above that, controlling that, is another spirit—the spirit which has made this undoubtedly the greatest shop in the world. I cannot describe it, but it exists. All my managers, and even many of the rank and file, feel it.'

'Very interesting,' said the lawyer.

'Mr. Polycarp,' Hugo announced solemnly, 'the direction of this establishment is my life. In the midst of this lovely and interesting organism I enjoy every hour of the day. What else can I want?'

Polycarp raised his eyebrows.

'Do you suppose it would add to my fun to have a million in the bank—I, with an income of two thousand a week? Do you suppose I should find it diverting to be at the beck and call of a board of directors—I, the supreme fount of authority? Do you suppose it would be my delight to consider eternally the interests of a pack of shareholders—I, who consider nothing but my fancy? And, finally, do you suppose it would amuse me, Hugo, to have "limited" put after my name? Me, limited!'

'Then,' said the lawyer slowly, 'I am to understand you are not willing—'

'My friend,' Hugo replied, dropping into his chair, 'I would sooner see the whole blessed place fall like the Bastille than see it "limited."'

Polycarp rose in his turn.

'My clients,' he remarked in a peculiar tone, 'had set their minds on this affair.'

'For once in a way your clients will be disappointed,' said Hugo.

'What do you mean—"for once in a way"?'

'Who are your clients, Mr. Polycarp?'

'Since the offer is rejected, it would be useless to divulge their names.'

'I will tell you, then,' said Hugo. 'Your client—for there is only one—is Louis Ravengar. I saw it stated in a paper the other day that Louis Ravengar had successfully floated thirty-nine companies with a total capitalization of thirty millions. But my scalp will not be added to his collection.'

'I shall not disclose the identity of my clients,' Mr. Polycarp minced. 'But, speaking of Mr. Ravengar, I have noticed that what he wants he gets. The manner in which the United Coal Company, Limited, was brought to flotation by him in the teeth of the opposition of the proprietors was really most interesting.'

'You mean to warn me that there are ways of compelling a private concern to become public and joint-stock?'

'Not at all, Mr. Hugo. I am incapable of such a hint. I am sure that nothing and nobody could force you against your will. I was only mentioning the case of the Coal Company. I could mention others.'

'Don't trouble, my dear sir. Convey my decision to Louis Ravengar, and give him my compliments. We are old acquaintances.'

'You are?' The solicitor seemed astonished in his imperturbable way.

'We are.'

'I will convey your decision to my clients.'

Accepting a cigar, Mr. Polycarp departed.

Without giving himself time to think, Hugo went straight to Department 42, and direct to the artist in hats. She stood pale and deferential to receive him. The heat was worse than ever.

'Your name is Payne, I think?' he began. (He well knew her name was Payne.)

'Yes, sir.'

Other employés in the trying-on room looked furtively round.

'About half-past eleven an old gentleman, with white moustache, came into this room, Miss Payne. You remember?'

'Yes, sir.'

'What did he want?'

'He was inquiring about a hat, sir,' she hurriedly answered.

'For a lady?'

'Yes, sir.'

'Thank you.'

And he hastened back to his central office, and breathed a sigh. 'I have actually spoken to her,' he murmured. 'How charming her voice is!'

But Miss Payne's physical condition desolated him. If she was so obviously exhausted at 12.30, what would she be like at the day's end?'

'I've got it!' he cried.

He seized a pen and wrote: 'Notice.—The public are respectfully informed that this establishment will close to-day at two o'clock.'

He rang a bell, and a messenger appeared.

'Take this to the printing-office instantly, and tell Mr. Waugh it must be posted throughout the place in half an hour.'

Shortly after two o'clock Sloane Street was amazed to witness the exodus of the three thousand odd. The closure was attributed to a whim of Hugo's for celebrating some obscure anniversary in his life. Many hundreds of persons were inconvenienced, and the internal economy of scores of polite homes seriously deranged. The evening papers found a paragraph. And Hugo lost perhaps a hundred and fifty pounds net. But Hugo was happy, and he was expectant.

At ten o'clock that night a youngish man, extremely like Simon Shawn, was brought by Simon into Hugo's presence under the dome. This was Simon's brother, Albert Shawn, a member of Hugo's private detective force.

'Sit down,' said Hugo. 'Well?'

'I reckon you've heard, sir,' Albert Shawn began impassively, 'the yarn that's going all round the stores.'

'I have not.'

'Everyone's whispering,' said Albert Shawn, gazing carefully at his boots, 'that Mr. Hugo has taken a kind of a fancy to Miss Payne.'

Hugo restrained himself.

'Heavens!' he exclaimed, with a clever affectation of lightness, 'what next? I've only spoken to the chit once.'

'Don't I know it, sir!'

'Enough of that! What have you to report?'

'Miss Payne left at 2.15, whipped round to the flats entrance, took the lift to the top-floor, went into Mr. Francis Tudor's flat.'

'What's that you say? Whose flat?' cried Hugo.

'Mr. Francis Tudor's, sir.'

Mr. Tudor was famous as the tenant of the suite rented at two thousand a year; he had a reputation for being artistic, sybaritic, and something in the inner ring of the City.

'Ah!' said Hugo. 'Perhaps she is a friend of one of Mr. Tudor's—'

'Servants,' he was about to say, but the idea of Miss Payne being on terms of equality with a menial was not pleasant to him, and he stopped.

'No, sir,' said Albert Shawn, unmoved. 'She is not, because Mr. Tudor shunted out all his servants soon afterwards. Miss Payne was shown into his study. She had her tea there, and her dinner. The Hugo half-guinea dinner was ordered late by telephone for two persons, and rushed up at eight o'clock.'

'I wonder Mr. Tudor didn't order an orchestra with the dinner,' said Hugo grimly. It was a sublime effort on his part to be his natural self.

'I waited for Miss Payne to leave,' continued Albert Shawn. 'That's why I'm so late.'

'And what time did she leave?'

'She hasn't left,' said Albert Shawn.

CHAPTER IV

CAMILLA

Hugo dismissed Albert, with orders to continue his vigil, and then he rang for Simon.

'Do you think I might have some tea?' he asked.

'I am disposed to think you might, sir,' said Simon the cellarer. 'It is eight days since you indulged after dinner.'

'Bring me one cup, then, poured out.'

He was profoundly disturbed by Albert's news. He was, in fact, miserable. He had a physical pain in the region of the heart. He wished he could step off Love as one steps off an omnibus, but he found that Love resembled an express train more than an omnibus.

'Can she be secretly married to him?' he demanded half aloud, sipping at the tea.

The idea soothed him exactly as much as it alarmed him.

'The question is,' he murmured angrily, 'am I or am I not an ass?... At my age!'

He felt vaguely that he was not, that he was rather a splendid and Byronic figure in the grip of tremendous emotions.

Having regretfully finished the tea, he unlocked a bookcase, and picked out at random a volume of Boswell's 'Johnson.' It was the modern Oxford edition—the only edition worthy of a true amateur—bound by Rivière. Like all wise and lettered men, Hugo consulted Boswell in the grave crises of life, and to-night he happened upon the venerable Johnson's remark: *'Sir, I would be content to spend the remainder of my existence driving about in a post-chaise with a pretty woman.'*

He leaned back in his chair and laughed. 'In the whole history of mankind,' he asserted to the dome, 'there have only been two really sensible men. Solomon was one, and Johnson the other.'

He restored the book to its place, and sat down to the piano-player, and in a moment the overture to 'Tannhäuser,' that sublime failure to prove that passion is folly, filled the vast apartment. The rushing violin passages, and every call of Aphrodite, intoxicated his soul and raised his spirits till he knew with the certainty of a fully-aroused instinct that Camilla Payne must be his. He became optimistic on all points.

'A lady insists on seeing you, sir,' said Simon Shawn, intruding upon the Pilgrims' Chant.

'She may insist,' Hugo answered lightly. 'But it all depends who she is. I'm—'

He stopped, for the insisting lady had entered.

It was Camilla.

He jumped up. Never before in his career had he been so astounded, staggered, charmed, enchanted, dazzled, and completely silenced.

'Miss Payne?' he gasped after a prolonged pause.

Simon Shawn effaced himself.

'Yes, Mr. Hugo.'

'Won't you sit down?'

The singular prevalence of beautiful women in England is only appreciated properly by Englishmen who have lived abroad, and these alone know also that in no other country is beauty wasted by women as it is wasted in England. Camilla was beautiful, and supremely beautiful; she was tall, well and generously formed, graceful, fair, with fine eyes and fine dark chestnut hair; her absolutely regular features had the proud Tennysonian cast. But the coldness of Tennysonian damsels was not hers. Whether she had Latin blood in her veins, or whether Nature had peculiarly gifted her out of sheer caprice, she possessed in a high degree that indescribable demeanour, at once a defiance and a surrender, a question and an answer, a confession and a denial, which is the universal weapon of women of Latin race in the battle of the sexes, but of which Englishwomen seem to be almost deprived. 'I am Eve!' say the mocking, melting eyes of the Southern woman, and so said Camilla's eyes. No man could rest calm under that glance; no man could forbear the attempt to decipher the hidden secrecies of its message, and no man could succeed in the task.

Hugo felt that he had never seen this woman before.

And he might have been excused for feeling so; for instead of the black alpaca, Camilla now wore a simple but effectively charming toilette such as 'Hugo's' created and sold to women for the rapture of men in summer twilights, and over the white dress was thrown a very rich pearl-tinted opera-cloak, which only partly concealed the curves of the shoulders, and poised aslant on the glistening coiffure was the identical blue hat with its wide brims that had visited the dome seventeen hours before. The total effect was calculated, perfect, overwhelming.

'I'm sorry to disturb you, Mr. Hugo,' said Camilla, throwing back her cloak on the left side with a fine gesture, 'but I am in need of your assistance.'

'Yes?' Hugo whispered, seating himself.

She had a low voice, rare in a blonde, and it thrilled him. And she was so near him in the great chamber!

'I want you to tell me what plot I am in the midst of. What is the web that has begun to surround me?'

'Plot?' stammered Hugo. 'Web?'

Her eyes flashed scrutinizingly on his face.

'You have a kind heart,' she said; 'everybody can see that. Be frank. Do you know,' she asked in a different tone, 'or don't you, that you spoke very gruffly to me this morning?'

'Miss Payne,' he began, 'I assure you—'

'I thought perhaps you didn't know,' she smiled calmly. 'But you did speak very gruffly. Now, I have taken my courage in both hands in order to come to you to-night. I may have lost my situation through it—I can't tell. Whether I have lost my situation or not, I appeal to you for candour.'

'Miss Payne,' said Hugo, 'it distresses me to hear you speak of a "situation."'

'And why?'

'You know why,' he answered. 'A woman as distinguished as you are must be perfectly well aware how distinguished she is, and perfectly capable, let me add, of hiding her distinction from the common crowd. For what purpose of your own you came into my shop, I can't guess. But necessity never forced you there. No doubt you meant to avoid getting yourself talked about; nevertheless, you have got yourself talked about.'

'Indeed!' She looked at him sideways.

'Yes,' Hugo went on; 'several thousands of commonplace persons are saying that I have fallen in love with you. Do you think it's true, this rumour?'

'How can I tell you?' said she.

'Well, it is true!' he cried. 'It's doubly and trebly true! It's the greatest truth in the world at the present moment. It is one of those truths that a believer can't keep to himself.' He paused, expectant. 'A woman less fine than you would have protested against this sudden avowal, which is only too like me—too like Hugo. You don't protest. I knew you wouldn't. I knew you knew. You asked for candour. You have it. I love you.'

'Then, why,' she demanded firmly, with a desolating smile—'why do you have me followed by your private detective?'

Hugo was caught in a trap. He had hesitated long before instructing Albert Shawn to shadow Camilla, but in the end his desire for exact knowledge concerning her, and his possession of a corps of detectives ready to hand, had proved too much for his scruples. He had, however, till that day discovered little of importance for his pains—merely that her parents, who were dead, had kept a small milliner's shop in Edgware Road, that her age was twenty-five, that she had come to his millinery department with a good testimonial from an establishment in Walham Green, that she lived in lodgings at Fulham and saw scarcely anyone, and that she had once been a typewriter.

'The fact is—'

He stopped, perceiving that the 'fact' would not do at all, and that to explain to the woman you love why you have spied on her is a somewhat nice operation.

'Is that the way you usually serve us?' pursued Camilla, with a strange emphasis on the word 'us' which maddened him.

'The fact is, Miss Payne,' he said boldly, sitting down as soon as he had invented the solution of the difficulty, 'you will not deny that this afternoon and this evening you have been in a position of some slight delicacy. What your relations are with Mr. Francis Tudor I have never sought to inquire, but I have always doubted the bonâ fides of Mr. Francis Tudor. And to-day I have simply—if I may say so—watched over you. If my man has been clumsy, I beg your forgiveness. I beg you to believe in my deep respect for you.'

The plain sincerity of his accent and of his gaze touched and convinced her. She looked at her feet, white-shod on the crimson carpet.

'Ah!' she murmured, as if to herself, mournfully, 'why don't you ask me how it is that I, to whom you pay thirty-six shillings a week, am wearing these clothes? Surely you must think that an employé who—'

'At this hour you are not an employé,' he interrupted here. 'You visit me of your own free will to demand an explanation of matters which are quite foreign to our business relations. I give it you. Beyond that I permit myself no thoughts except such as any man is entitled to concerning any woman. You used the word "plot" when you came in. What did you refer to? If Mr. Tudor has—' He could not proceed.

'As I left Mr. Tudor's flat a few minutes since,' said Camilla quietly, producing a revolver from the folds of her cloak, 'I picked up this. It may or may not be loaded. Perhaps you can tell me.'

He seized the weapon, and impetuously aimed at a heavy Chinese gong across the room, and pulled the trigger several times. The revolver spoke noisily, and the gong sounded and swung.

'You see!' he exclaimed. 'Pardon the din. I did it without thinking.'

'Did you call, sir?' asked Simon Shawn, appearing in the doorway.

Hugo extirpated him with a look.

'How cool you are!' he resumed to Camilla, and laid down the revolver. 'No, you aren't! By Jove, you aren't! What is it? What have you been through? What is this plot? A plot—in my building—and against you! Tell me everything—everything! I insist.'

'Shall you believe all that I say?' she ventured.

'Yes,' he said, 'all.'

He saw with intense joy that he was going to be friendly with her. It seemed too good to be true.

CHAPTER V

A STORY AND A DISAPPEARANCE

'Perhaps I ought to begin by informing you,' said Camilla Payne, 'that I have known Mr. Francis Tudor for about two years. Always he has been very nice to me. Once he asked me to marry him—quite suddenly—it was a year ago. I refused because I didn't care for him. I then saw nothing of him for some time. But after I entered your service here, he came across me again by accident. I did not know until lately that he had one of your flats. He was very careful, very polite, timid, cautious—but very obstinate, too. He invited me to call on him at his rooms, and to bring any friends I liked. Of course, it was a stupidity on his part, but, then, what else could he do? A man who wants to cultivate relations with a homeless shopgirl is rather awkwardly fixed.'

'I wish to Heaven you would not talk like that, Miss Payne!' said Hugo, interrupting her impatiently.

'I am merely telling you these things so that you may understand my position,' Camilla coldly replied. 'Do you imagine that I am amusing myself?'

'Go on, go on, I beg,' he urged, with a gesture of apology.

'Naturally, I declined the invitation. Then next I received a letter from him, in which he said that unless I called on him, or agreed to meet him in some place where we could talk privately and at length, he should kill himself within a week. And he added that death was perhaps less to him than I imagined. I believed that letter. There was something about it that touched me.'

'And so you decided to yield?'

'I did yield. I felt that if I was to trust him at all, I might as well trust him fully, and I called at his flat this afternoon alone. He was evidently astonished to see me at that hour, so I explained to him that you had closed early for some reason or other.'

'Exactly,' said Hugo.

He insisted on giving me tea. I was treated, in fact, like a princess; but during tea he said nothing to me that might not have been said before a roomful of people. After tea he left me for a few moments, in order, as he said, to give some orders to his servants. Up till then he had been extremely agitated, and when he returned he was even more agitated. He walked to and fro in that lovely drawing-room of his—just as you were doing here not long since. I was a little afraid.'

'Afraid of what?' demanded Hugo.

'I don't know—of him, lest he might do something fatal, irretrievable; something—I don't know. And then, being alone with him in that palace of a place! Well, he burst out suddenly into a series of statements about himself, and about his future, and his intentions, and his feelings towards me. And these statements were so extraordinary and so startling that I could not think he had invented them. I believed them, as I had believed in the sincerity of his threat to kill himself if I would not listen to him.'

'And what were they—these statements?' Hugo inquired.

Camilla waved aside the interruptions, and continued: '"Now," he said, "will you marry me? Will you marry me now?"'

She paused and glanced at Hugo, who observed that her eyes were filling with tears.

'And then?' murmured Hugo soothingly.

'Then I agreed to marry him.'

And with these words she cried openly.

'If anyone had told me beforehand,' she resumed, 'that I should be so influenced by a man's —a man's acting, I would have laughed. But I was—I was. He succeeded completely.'

'You have not said what these extraordinary statements were,' Hugo insisted.

'Don't ask me,' she entreated, drying her eyes. 'It is enough that I was hoodwinked. If you have had no hand in this plot, don't ask me. I am too ashamed, too scornful of my credulity, to repeat them. You would laugh.'

'Should I?' said Hugo, smiling gravely. 'What occurred next?'

'The next step was that Mr. Tudor asked me to accompany his housekeeper to the housekeeper's room, and on the other side of the passage from the drawing-room I was to dine with him. The housekeeper is a Mrs. Dant, a kind, fat, lame old woman, and she produced this cloak and this hat, and so on, and said that they were for me! I was surprised, but I praised them and tried them on for a moment. You must remember that I was his affianced wife. I talked with Mrs. Dant, and prepared myself for dinner, and then I went back to the drawing-room, and found Mr. Tudor ready for dinner. I asked him why he had got the clothes, and he said he had got them this very morning merely on the chance of my accepting his proposal out of pity for him. And I believed that, too.'

There was a silence.

'But that is not the end?' Hugo encouraged her.

'Oh,' she exclaimed, 'it is useless, all this story! And the episode is finished! When I came in here I was angry; I suspect you of some complicity. But I suspect you no longer, and I see now that the wisest course for a woman such as I after such an adventure is to be mute about it, and to forget it.'

'No,' he said; 'you are wrong. Trust me. I entreat.'

Camilla bit her lip.

'We went into the dining-room, and dinner was served,' she recommenced, 'and there I had my first shock, my first doubt, for one of the two waiters was your spy.'

'Shawn! My detective!'

Hugo was surprised to find that Albert, almost a novice in his vocation, had contrived to be so insinuating.

'And he made a very bad waiter indeed,' Camilla added.

'I regret it,' said Hugo. 'He meant well.' 'When the waiters had gone I asked Mr. Tudor if they were his own servants. He hesitated, and then admitted frankly that they were not. He told me that his servants were out on leave for the evening. "You don't mean to say that I am now alone with you in the flat!" I protested. "No," he said quickly. "Mrs. Dant is always in her room across the passage. Don't be alarmed, dearest." His tone reassured me. After coffee, he took my photograph by flashlight. He printed one copy at once, and then, after we had both been in the dark-room together, he returned there to get some more printing-paper. While he was absent I went into the housekeeper's room for a handkerchief which I had left there. Mrs. Dant was not in the room. But in a mirror I saw the reflection of a man hiding behind the door. I was awfully frightened. However, I pretended to see nothing, and tried to hum a song. I same into the passage. The passage window was open, and I looked out. Another man was watching on the balcony. Of course, I saw instantly it was a plot. I—I—'

'Did you recognise the men, then?' Hugo asked.

'The one in the room I was not quite sure of. The other, on the balcony, was your detective, I think. I saw him disappear in this direction.'

'But whatever the plot was, Shawn had no hand in it.'

'No, no, of course not! I see now. But the other, in the room! Ah, if you knew all my history, you would understand better! I felt that some vengeance was out against me. I saw everything clearly. I tried to keep my head, and to decide calmly what I ought to do. It was from a little table in the passage that I picked up the revolver. Then I heard hurried footsteps coming through the drawing-room towards the passage. It was Mr. Tudor. He seemed very startled. I tried to appear unconcerned. "What is the matter?" he asked; he had gone quite pale. "Nothing," I said. "I only went to fetch a handkerchief." He laughed uneasily. "I was afraid you had thought better of it and run away from me," he said. And he kissed me; I was obliged to submit. All this time I was thinking hard what to do. I suggested we should go on to the roof garden for awhile. He objected, but finally he gave way, and he brought me the cloak and hat, and we went to the garden and sat down. I felt safer there. At last I ventured to tell him that I must go home. Of course, he objected to that too, but he gave way a second time. "I will just speak to Mrs. Dant," I said. "You stay here for three minutes. By that time I shall be ready." And I went off towards the flat, but as soon as I was out of his sight I turned and ran here. And that's all.'

'You are a wonderful creature,' Hugo murmured, looking at her meditatively.

'Why?' The question was put with a sort of artless and melancholy surprise.

'How can I tell?' said Hugo. 'How can I tell why Heaven made you so?'

She laughed, and the laugh enchanted him. He had studied her during her recital; he had observed her continual effort to use ordinary words and ordinary tones like a garment to hide vivid sensations and emotions which, however, shone through the garment as her face might have shone through a veil.

He recalled her little gestures, inflections, glances—the thousand avenues by which her rich and overflowing individuality escaped from the prison of her will, and impressed itself on the rest of the created universe. Her story was decidedly singular, and as mysterious as it was singular; that something sinister would be brought to light, he felt sure. But what occupied and charmed his mind was the exquisite fact that between him and her relations were now established. The story, her past danger, even her possible future danger—these things only interested him in so far as they formed the basis of an intimacy. He exulted in being near her, in the savour of her commanding presence. When he thought of her in his monstrous shop, wilting in the heat, bowing deferentially to fools, martyrizing her soul for less than two pounds a week, he thought of kings' daughters sold into slavery. But she was a princess now, and for evermore, and she had come to him of her own free will; she had trusted him; she had invited his help! It was glorious beyond the dreams of his passion.

'Come,' he said feverishly, 'show me how you managed to get to my dome.'

And he threw open the easternmost window, and she stepped with him out on to the balcony.

They looked down across Hugo's little private garden, into the blackness of the court of fountains, whose balconies were vaguely disclosed here and there by the reflection from lit interiors. On the other side of the deep pit of the court was the vast expanse of flat roof containing the famous roof garden. Amid dwarf trees and festoons of coloured lights, the figures of men and women who counted themselves the cream of London could dimly be seen walking about or sitting at tables; and the wild strain of the Tsigane musicians, as they swayed to and fro in their red coats on the bandstand, floated towards the dome through the heavy summer air. In the near distance the fantastic shapes of chimney-cowls raised themselves against the starry but moonless sky, and miles away the grandiose contours of a dome far greater than Hugo's—the dome of St. Paul's—finished the prospect in solemn majesty. It was a scene well calculated to intensify a man's emotions, especially when a man stands to view it, as Hugo stood, on a lofty balcony, with a beautiful and loved woman by his side.

She was indicating pathways, as well as she could, when they both saw a man hurrying in the direction of the dome along by the roof-balustrade of the court of fountains—the route by which Camilla herself had come. He arrived under the dome, and would have disappeared into a doorway had not Hugo called:

'Shawn, I'm here!'

'I was just coming to see you, sir,' replied Albert Shawn in a loud whisper, as he climbed breathless up to the little raised garden beneath the dome.

Camilla withdrew behind a curtain of the window.

'Well?' Hugo queried.

'She's gone, sir. But dashed if I know where, unless she's got herself lost somewhere on the roof.'

'She is here,' said Hugo, lowering his voice. 'And it appears that you waited very clumsily at that dinner, my boy. A bad disguise is worse than none. I must lend you Gaboriau's "Crime of Orcival" to read; that will teach you. Anything else to tell me?'

'I went back to the balcony entrance of the flat,' the youthful detective replied humbly, looking up to Hugo in the window of the dome. 'I could see through the lacework of the blind; the drawing-room was empty. The French window was open an inch or so, and I could hear a clock ticking as clear as a bell. Then Mr. Tudor toddled up, and I hid in the servants' doorway. Mr. Tudor went in by the other door, and out I popped again to my post. I see my gentleman stamping about and calling "Camilla! Camilla!" fit to burst. No answer. Then he picks up a photograph off a table and kisses it smack—twice.'

Camilla stirred behind the curtain.

'Then he goes into another room,' proceeded Albert Shawn, 'and lo and behold! another man comes from round the corner of a screen—a man much older than Mr. Tudor! And Mr. Tudor runs in again, and these two meet—these two do. And they stare at each other, and Mr. Tudor says, "Hullo, Louis—"'

'I knew it!' The cry came from Camilla within the dome.

'What?' demanded Hugo, turning to her and ignoring Shawn.

'It was Louis Ravengar whom I saw hiding behind the door. I felt all the time that it was he!'

And she put her hands to her face.

'Ravengar!' He was astounded to hear that name. What had she, what had Tudor, to do with Ravengar?

'That was why I thought *you* were in the plot, Mr. Hugo,' she added.

'Me? Why?'

'Can you ask?'

Her eyes met his, and it was his that fell.

'I have no relations whatever with Ravengar, I assure you,' he said gravely. 'But, by the dagger! I'll see this affair to the end.' 'By the dagger' was a form of oath, meaningless yet terrible in sound, which Hugo employed only on the greatest occasions. He turned sharply to the window. 'Anything else, Shawn?'

'There was a gust of wind that shut the blessed window, sir. I couldn't hear any more, so I came to report.'

'Go to the front entrance of the flat instantly,' Hugo ordered him. 'I will watch the balcony.'

'Yes, sir.'

Camilla was crouching in the embrasure of the window. Her body seemed to shake.

'There is nothing to fear,' Hugo soothed her. 'Stay here till I return.' And he snatched up the revolver.

'No,' she said, straightening herself; 'I must go with you.'

'Better not.'

'I must go with you,' she repeated.

They passed together along the railed edge of the court of fountains under the stars, skirted the gay and melodious garden behind the trees in their huge wooden boxes, and so came to a second quadrangle, upon whose highest story the windows of Tudor's flat gave. Descending a stairway of forged iron to the balcony, they crept forward in silence to the window of Tudor's drawing-room, and, still side by side, gazed, as Shawn had done, through the fine lacework of the blind into the splendid apartment.

The window was almost at a corner of the room, near a door; but Hugo had a perfect view of the two men within, and one was as certainly Louis Ravengar as the other was Francis Tudor. They were gesticulating violently and angrily, and a heavy, ornate Empire chair had already been overturned. The dispute seemed to be interminable; each moment heralded a fight, but it is the watched pot that never boils. Suddenly Hugo became aware that Camilla was no longer at his elbow, and the next instant, to his extreme amazement, he saw her glide into the room. She had removed her hat and cloak, and stood revealed in all her beauty. The two men did not perceive her. She softly opened the window, and the confused murmur of voices reached Hugo's ear.

'Give me the revolver,' Camilla whispered.

And her whisper was such that he passed the weapon, as it were hypnotically, to her under the blind. And then the blind slipped down, and he could see no more. He heard a shot, and the next thing was that the revolver was pushed back to him, nearly at the level of the floor.

'Wait there!' The sound of her voice, tense and authoritative, came through the slit of the window and thrilled him. 'All is well now, but I will send you a message.'

And the window was swiftly closed and a curtain drawn behind the blind. He could hear nothing.

He had small intention of obeying her. 'She must have gone in by the servants' entrance,' he argued. 'I should have seen her if she had tried the other.' And he ran to the small door, but it was shut fast. In vain he knocked and shook the handle for several minutes. Then he hastened to the main door on the broad balcony, but that also was impregnable.

Should he break a pane?

A noise far along the balcony attracted him. He flew towards it, found nothing but a cat purring, and returned. The luscious music of the Tsigane band, one of the nine orchestras which he owned, reached him faintly over the edge of the quadrangle.

Then he decidedly did hear human footsteps on the balcony. They were the footsteps of Shawn.

'She's gone, sir. Took the lift, and whizzed off in Mr. Tudor's electric brougham that was waiting.'

'And the men?' he gasped.

'Seen neither of them, sir. She put this note in my hand as she passed me, sir.'

CHAPTER VI

A LAPSE FROM AN IDEAL

'If you please, sir,' said Simon Shawn, when he brought Hugo's tea the next morning, 'I am informed that a man has secreted himself on the summit of the dome.'

Hugo, lying moveless on his back, and ignoring even the tea, made no reply to this speech. He was still repeating to himself the following words, which, by constant iteration, had assumed in his mind the force and emphasis of italics: *'So grateful for your sympathetic help. When next I see you, if there is opportunity, I will try to thank you. Meantime, all is well with me. Please trouble no more. And forget.'* Such were the exact terms of the note from Camilla Payne delivered to him by Albert Shawn. Of course, he knew it by heart. It was scribbled very hastily in pencil on half a sheet of paper, and it bore no signature, not even a solitary initial. If it had not been handed to Albert by Camilla in person, Hugo might have doubted its genuineness, and might have spent the night in transgressing the law of trespass and other laws, in order to be assured of a woman's safety. But under the circumstances he could not doubt its genuineness. What he doubted was its exact import. And what he objected to in it was its lack of information. He wished ardently to know whether Ravengar and Tudor, or either of them, had been wounded, and if so, by whose revolver; for he could not be certain that it was Camilla who had fired. An examination of the revolver which he and she had passed from hand to hand had shown two chambers undischarged. He wished ardently to know how she had contrived to settle her account with Tudor, and yet get away in Tudor's brougham, unless it was by a wile worthy of the diplomacy of a Queen Elizabeth. And he wished ardently to understand a hundred and one other things concerning Camilla, Tudor, and Ravengar, and the permutations and combinations of these three, which offered apparently insoluble problems to his brain. Nevertheless, there was one assurance which seemed to him to emerge clearly from the note, and to atone for its vagueness—a vagueness, however, perfectly excusable, he reflected, having regard to the conditions in which it was written—namely, that Camilla intended to arrive, as usual, in Department 42 that morning. What significance could be attached to the phrase, 'When next I see you,*if there is opportunity*,' unless it signified that she anticipated seeing him next in the shop and in the course of business? Moreover, he felt that it would be just like Camilla to start by behaving to him as though nothing had occurred. (But he would soon alter that, he said masterfully.) He was, on the whole, happy as he lay in bed. She knew that he loved her. They had been intimate. In three hours at most he would see her again. And his expectations ran high. Indeed, she had already begun to exist in his mind as his life's companion.

Simon coughed politely but firmly.

'What's that you say?' Hugo demanded; and Simon repeated his item of news.

'Ha!' said Hugo; 'doubtless some enthusiast for sunrises.'

'He has been twice perceived in the little gallery by the men cleaning the roof garden,' Simon added.

'And who is it?'

'His identity has not been established,' said Simon.

'Can't you moderate your language a little, Shawn?' Hugo asked, staring always absently up into the dome.

'I beg pardon, sir. I have spent part of the night with Albert, and his loose speech always drives me to the other extreme,' Simon observed, repentant.

'Has Albert seen the burglar?'

'No, sir, if it *is* a burglar.'

'Well,' said Hugo, 'he's quite safe where he is. He can't get down except by that door, can he?' pointing to a masked door, which was painted to represent a complete set in sixty volumes of the 'Acts of the Saints.'

'No, sir.'

'And he could only have got up by that door?' Hugo pursued.

'Yes, sir.'

'Which means that you were away from your post last night, my son.'

'I was, sir,' Shawn admitted frankly. 'When you and Albert and the lady ran off so quickly, I followed, as far as I judged expedient—beg pardon, sir. The man must have slipped in during my absence. I remember I noticed the masked door was ajar on my return. I shut and locked it.'

'That explains everything,' said Hugo. 'You see how your sins find you out.'

'Yes, sir.'

'I say, Shawn,' Hugo cried, as he went to his bath, 'talking of that chap up above, play me the Captives' chorus from "Fidelio."'

'It is not in the répertoire, sir,' said Simon, after searching.

'Not in the répertoire! Impossible!'

'No, sir.'

'Ah well, then, let us have the Wedding March from "Lohengrin."'

'With pleasure, sir.'

But Simon was unfortunate that morning. The toilet completed, Hugo came towards him swinging the gold token, the bearer of which had the right to take whatever he chose from all the hundred and thirty-one departments of the stores in exchange for a simple receipt.

'I will interview the burglar,' said Hugo. 'But just run down first and get me a pair of handcuffs.'

In ten minutes Simon returned crestfallen.

'We do not keep handcuffs, sir,' he stammered.

'Not—keep—! What nonsense! First you tell me that "Fidelio" is not in the répertoire, and then you have the effrontery to add that we do not keep handcuffs. Shawn, are you not aware that the fundamental principle of this establishment is that we keep everything? If we received an order for a herd of white elephants—'

'No doubt our arrangement with Jamrach's would enable us to supply them, sir,' Simon put in rapidly. 'But handcuffs seem to be a monopoly of the State.'

'Evidently, Shawn, you are not familiar with the famous remark of Louis the Fourteenth.'

'I am not, sir.'

'He said, "*L'état, c'est moi.*" Show me the catalogue.'

Simon, bearing on his shoulders at that moment the sins of ten managers, scurried to bring an immense tome, bound in crimson leather, and inscribed in gold, 'Hugo, General Catalogue.' It contained nearly two thousand large quarto pages, and above six thousand illustrations. Hugo turned solemnly to the exhaustive index, which alone occupied seventy pages of small type, and, running his finger down a column, he read out, Handbells, handbell-ringers, handbills, hand-embroidered sheets, handkerchiefs, handles, handsaws, hansoms, Hardemann's beetle powder, hares, haricot beans....'

'Lamentable!' he ejaculated—'lamentable! You will tell Mr.—Mr. Banbury this morning to procure some handcuffs, assorted sizes, at once, and to add them to the—the—Explorers' Outfit Department.'

'Precisely, sir.'

'In the meantime I shall have to ascend the dome, and face the burglar without this necessary of life. Give me the revolver instead.'

CHAPTER VII

POSSIBLE ESCAPE OF SECRETS

The top of the dome was fashioned into a kind of belvedere, with a small circular gallery. Hugo emerged at the head of the stairs, and saw no living thing; but at the sound of his footstep a man sprang nervously into view round the curve of the gallery, and fronted him.

Hugo, with his hands still on either rail of the staircase, took the top step, gazing the while at his burglar, first in wonder, and then with a capricious abandonment to what he considered the humour of the situation. He thought of Albert Shawn's account of the meeting between Francis Tudor and his visitor in Tudor's flat on the previous night, and some fantastic impulse, due to the strain of Welsh blood in him, caused him to address the man as Tudor had addressed him:

'Hullo, Louis!'

There was a pause, and then came the reply in a tone which might have been ferocious or facetious:

'Well, my young friend?'

It was indeed Louis Ravengar. Dishevelled, fatigued, and unstrung, he formed a sinister contrast to Hugo, fresh from repose, cold water and music, and also to the spirit of the beautiful summer morning itself, which at that unspoilt hour seemed always to sojourn for a space in the belvedere. The sun glinted joyously on the golden ornament of the dome, and on Hugo's smooth hair, but it revealed without pity the stains on Ravengar's flaccid collar and the disorder of his evening clothes and opera-hat.

He was a fairly tall man, with thin gray hair round the sides of his head, but none on the crown nor on his face, the chief characteristics of which were the square jaw, the extremely long upper lip, the flat nose, and the very small blue-gray eyes. He looked sixty, and was scarcely fifty. He looked one moment like a Nonconformist local preacher who had mistaken his vocation; but he was nothing of the kind. He looked the next moment like a good hater and a great scorner of scruples; and he was.

These two men had not exchanged a word, had not even seen each other, save at the rarest intervals, for nearly a quarter of a century. They were the principals in a quarrel of the most vivid, satanic, and incurable sort known to anthropological science—the family quarrel—and the existence of this feud was a proof of the indisputable truth that it sometimes takes less than two to make a quarrel. For, though Owen Hugo was not absolutely an angel, Ravengar had made it single-handed.

The circumstances of its origin were quite simple. When Louis Ravengar was nine years old, his father, a widower, married a widow with one child, aged six. That child was Hugo. The two lads, violently different in temperament—the one gloomy and secretive, the other buoyant and frank—with no tie of blood or of affection, were forced by destiny to grow up together in the same house, and by their parents even to sleep in the same room. They were never apart, and they loathed each other. Louis regarded young Owen as an interloper, and acted towards him as boys and tigers will towards interlopers weaker than themselves. The mischief was that Owen, in course of years, became a great favourite with his step-father. This roused Louis to a fury which was the more dangerous in that Owen had begun to overtake him in strength, and the fury could, therefore, find no outlet. Then Owen's mother died, and Ravengar, senior, married again—a girl this time, who soon discovered that the household in which she had planted herself was far too bellicose to be comfortable. She abandoned her husband, and sought consolation and sympathy with another widower, who also was blessed with offspring. Such is the foolishness of women. You cannot cure a woman of being one. But it must be said in favour of the third Mrs. Ravengar and her consoler that they conducted their affair with praiseworthy attention to outward decency. She went to America by one steamer, and purchased a divorce in Iowa for two hundred dollars. He followed in the next steamer, and they were duly united in Minneapolis. Meanwhile, the Ravengar household, left to the ungoverned passions of three males, became more and more impossible, and at length old Ravengar expired. In his will he stated that it was only from a stern sense of justice that he divided his considerable fortune in equal shares between Louis and Owen. Had he consulted his inclination, he would have left one shilling to Louis, and the remainder to Owen, who alone had been a true son to him.

It was a too talkative will. Testators, like politicians, should never explain.

Louis, who got as a favour half the fortune of which the whole was, in his opinion, his by right, was naturally exasperated in the highest degree by the terms of the indiscreet testament, and on the day of the funeral he parted from the son of his step-mother, swearing, in a somewhat melodramatic manner, that he would be revenged. Hugo was then twenty-one, and for twenty-five years he had waited in vain for symptoms of the revenge.

And now they met again, in the truest sense strangers. And each had a reason for humouring the other, for each wanted to know what the other had to do with Camilla Payne.

'So you're determined, Louis,' said Hugo lightly, 'to bring me to my knees about the transfer of my business to a limited company, eh?'

'What on earth do you mean, man?' asked Ravengar, whose voice was always gruff.

'I refer to Polycarp's visit yesterday.'

'I know nothing of it,' said Ravengar slowly, looking across the wilderness of roofs.

'Then why are you here, Louis? Is your revenge at last matured?'

Ravengar controlled himself, and glanced round as if for unseen aid in a forlorn enterprise.

'Owen,' he said, moved, 'I'm here because I need your help. I won't say anything about the past. I know you were always good-natured. And you've worn better than I have. I need your help in a matter of supreme importance to me. I became aware last night that you and your men were interested in the proceedings at Tudor's flat. I ran here, meaning to see you. There was no one in the big circular room downstairs, and no one at the entrance. Then I saw your servant coming, and I retreated through the door. I wished my presence to be known only to you. The door was locked on me. I knocked in vain. Then I stumbled up the stairs, and found myself out here. I wanted to calm myself, and here I remained. I knew your habit of coming up here at early morning. That is the whole explanation of my presence.'

Hugo nodded.

'I guessed as much,' he said. 'I will help you if I can. But first tell me what happened in the flat last night after Miss Payne entered while you and Tudor were quarrelling. She fired on you?'

'No,' said Ravengar; 'I believe she would have done. It was Tudor who drew a revolver and fired. Had I had my own—But I had laid it on a table, like a fool, and it disappeared.'

'Is not this it?' asked Hugo, producing Camilla's weapon.

Ravengar nodded, amazed.

'I thought so,' Hugo said, and returned it to his pocket. 'Were you wounded?'

'It was nothing. A scratch on the wrist. See! But I left. She—she ordered me to. And I saw I had no chance. I came out by the principal door on the balcony while you were struggling with the servants' door.'

'Wait a moment,' Hugo put in. 'Tudor knew you were hiding in the flat?'

'Not much!' exclaimed Ravengar. 'I dropped on him like something out of the sky. It cost me some trouble to get in. I had a silly old housekeeper to dispose of.'

Hugo's heart fell.

'Great heavens!' he sighed.

'Why? What's the matter?'

'Nothing. But tell me what you wanted to get into the flat for at all. What is there between you and Tudor?'

'Man! he's taken Camilla from me!' The accents of rage and despair were in Ravengar's voice as he uttered these words. 'He's taken her from me! She was my typewriter, you know. I fell in love with her. We were engaged!'

Hugo was startled for a moment; then he smiled bitterly and incredulously. It seemed too monstrous and absurd that Camilla should have betrothed herself to this forbidding, ugly, ageing, and terrible man.

'You were engaged? Never! Perhaps you aren't aware that she was engaged to Tudor?'

'I tell you we were engaged.'

'She accepted you?'

'Why not? I meant well by the girl.'

'And then she disappeared?'

Hugo spoke with a certain cynicism.

'How do you know?' Ravengar demanded angrily.

'I only guess.'

'Well, she did. I can't imagine why. I meant well by her. And the next thing is, I find her working in your shop, and in the arms of that scoundrel, Tudor.' He hesitated, and then, as he proceeded, his tones softened to an appeal. 'Owen, why were you watching last night? I must know. It's an affair of life or death to me.'

Hugo did not believe most of Ravengar's story, and he perceived the difficulty of his own position and the necessity for caution.

'I was watching because Miss Payne thought herself in some mysterious danger,' he said.

'She came to me, as you have done, to ask my help. And I won't hide from you that it was she herself who informed me definitely that Tudor had invited her to marry him, and that she had consented.'

'She shall not marry him!' cried Ravengar, exasperated.

'You are right,' said Hugo. 'She shall not. I have yet to be convinced even that he meant to marry her.'

'The rascal! He and I had business relations for several years before I discovered who he was. Of course, you know?'

'Indeed I don't,' said Hugo, 'if he isn't Francis Tudor.'

'He has as much right to the name of Tudor as you have to the name of Hugo,' Ravengar sneered. 'He is the son of the man who dishonoured my father's name by pretending to marry that woman in Minneapolis. Even if I hated my father, I've no cause to love *that* branch of our complicated family connections.'

Hugo whistled.

'I did not think there was so much money there,' he said at length.

'There wasn't. The fellow came into twenty thousand two years ago, and he has never earned a cent.'

'Yet he's living at the rate of five thousand a year at least.'

'It's like him!' Ravengar snorted. 'It's like him!'

'Perhaps he can't help it,' Hugo said queerly. 'Everyone isn't like you and me.'

'He can help robbing me of my future wife!'

'But she left you of her own accord.'

'Owen, she must marry me. It is essential. You must bring your influence to bear,' Ravengar burst out wildly. 'She must be my wife!'

'My dear fellow,' Hugo protested calmly, 'what are you dreaming of? I have no influence. You talk like a man at his wits' end.'

There was a silence.

'I am a man at his wits' end,' Ravengar murmured, half sadly. 'I trusted that girl. She knows all my secrets.'

'What secrets?' asked Hugo, struck by the phrase.

'My business secrets, of course. What else do you fancy?'

'My fancy is too active,' said Hugo, with careful casualness. 'It runs away with me. I was thinking of other sorts of secrets, and of that curious principle of English law that a wife can't give evidence against her husband.... You must pardon my fancy,' he added.

'Do you mean to insinuate that my eagerness to marry Camilla Payne is in order to prevent her from being able to—'

'No, Louis; I mean to insinuate nothing. Can't you see a joke?'

'I cannot,' said Ravengar. 'Not that variety of joke.'

'The appreciation of humour was never your strong point.'

Something in Hugo's manner made Ravengar spring forward; then he checked himself.

'Owen,' he entreated, 'don't let's quarrel again. I beg you to help me. Help me, and I'll promise never to interfere with you in your business—I'll swear it.'

'Then it was you, after all, that instructed Polycarp?'

Ravengar gave an affirmative sign.

'I meant either to get hold of this place or to ruin you. Remember what I suffered—in the old days.... You see I'm frank with you. Help me. We're neither of us growing younger. I'm mad for that girl, and I must have her.'

Hugo put his hands into his pockets, and consulted his toes. This semi-step-brother of his somehow aroused his compassion.

'No, Louis,' he said; 'I can't.'

'You hate me?'

'Not a bit.'

'Do you think I'm too old to marry, or what is it?'

'It's just like this, Louis, my friend: I have every intention of marrying Miss Payne myself.'

'You!... Ah!... Indeed!'

'I have so decided. And when I decide, the thing is as good as done.'

'And that's why you were watching last night! Good! Oh, good! Only I may as well inform you, Owen, that if Camilla Payne marries anyone but me, there will be murder. And no ordinary murder, either!'

Hugo took a turn in the gallery. He felt genuinely sorry for the gray and desperate man, driven by the intensity of emotion to utterances which were merely absurd.

'Louis,' he remarked, with a melancholy kindliness of tone, 'fate has a grudge against us two. It ruined our youth, and now it's embroiling us once more. Can't we both be philosophical? Can't we contrive to look at the thing in a—'

'Enough!' Ravengar almost yelled. 'You always talked that kind of d——d nonsense, you did! Unless you can arrange to say you'll give her up, you may as well hold your tongue.'

'Very well,' said Hugo, 'I'll hold my tongue.'

'That's all, then?'

'Quite all.'

'I suppose I can go? You'll let me pass? You'll not exercise your right to treat me as a burglar?'

'There are the stairs. Pass Shawn boldly. He is terrible, but he will not eat you.'

'Thanks.'

'And that is the unrivalled company promoter! And this is life!' Hugo meditated when he was alone on the dome.

He leaned over the railing of the gallery, and watched his legions gathering for the day's battle.

CHAPTER VIII

ORANGE-BLOSSOM

Some two hours later Hugo was in one of the common rooms devoted to the leisure and diversion of the legions in the upper basement: a large and bright apartment, ornamented with bookcases, wicker chairs, and reproductions of all that was most uplifting in graphic art. It was the domain of the ladies engaged in Departments 30 to 45, and was managed by an elected committee of their number. Affixed to the walls, in and out among the specimens of graphic art, were quite a lot of little red diamond squares, containing in white the words, 'Do it now,' in excessively readable letters. A staff notice about the early closing of the previous day had been pinned up near the door, and printed information relating to a trip to the Isle of Man, balloting for the use of motor-cars on Sundays, and a gratis book entitled 'Human Nature in Shoppers,' were also prominent. Above the fireplace was a fine mirror, and Hugo was personally engaged in pasting on the mirror a fine and effective poster, which ran as follows:

'Interesting. Last year the sales of the Children's Boot and Shoe Department surpassed the sales of the Ladies' Ditto by £558. In the first half of this year, on the contrary, the sales of the Ladies' Boot and Shoe Department have surpassed the sales of the Children's Ditto by £25. Great credit is due to the staff of the L.B. and S.D. But will the staff of the C.B. and S.D. allow themselves to be thus wiped out? That is the question, and Mr. Hugo will watch for the answer. Managers' Council, July 10th.'

Hugo, as the supreme head of Hugo's, had organized his establishment in such a manner as to leave no regular duties for himself, conformably to the maxim that a well-managed business is a business which runs smoothly and efficiently when the manager is not managing, and to that other maxim that the highest aim of the competent manager should be to make himself unnecessary. Hence he was perfectly at liberty to be wayward and freakish in his activities from time to time. And this happened to be one of his wayward and freakish mornings. There were, however, few young women in the common room to behold his aberration, for the hour was within two minutes of nine, and at nine o'clock the latest of the legionaries was supposed to be at her post. Three girls who were being hastily served with glasses of milk by a pink-aproned waitress politely feigned not to see him. Then another girl ran in, and she, too, had to pretend that the spectacle of Hugo pasting posters on mirrors was one of the most ordinary in life. Hugo glanced at this last comer in the mirror, and sighed a secret disappointment.

The interview with Louis Ravengar had left him less perturbed than might be imagined—at any rate, as regards Ravengar's own share in what had occurred and what was to occur. He was inclined to leave Ravengar out of the account, and to put the greater part of his hysterical appeals and threats down to the effect of a sleepless and highly unusual night. That Ravengar was absolutely sincere in his desire to marry Camilla he did not doubt, and he fully shared the frenzied man's determination that Camilla should not marry Francis Tudor. But beyond this Hugo did not go. He certainly did not go so far as to believe that Camilla had ever formally engaged herself to Ravengar. He thought it just possible that Ravengar might have committed a crime, or several crimes, and that Camilla might have knowledge of them, but the question whether Ravengar was or was not a criminal appeared to him to be a little off the point.

The unique point was his own prospects with Camilla. It may be said that he felt capable of shielding her from forty Ravengars.

He had torn prudence to shreds, and stamped on it, that morning, and had gone down boldly and directly to Department 42 at a quarter to nine, in order to meet Camilla. And she had not then arrived. He had then conceived the idea of, and the excuse for, a visit to the common room, through which every assistant was obliged to pass on her way to the receipt of custom. In the whole history of Hugo's a poster had never before been known to be posted on a mirror, which is utterly the wrong place for a poster, but Hugo had chosen the mirror as the field of his labours solely that he might surreptitiously observe every soul that entered the room.

The clock on the mantelpiece struck nine, and the last assistant had fled, and Hugo was left alone with the pink-aproned waitress, who was collecting glasses on a tray.

'Has Miss Payne come this morning?' he asked casually of the girl, patting the poster like an artist absorbed in his work.

It was a reckless question. He well knew that in half an hour the whole basement would be aware that Mr. Hugo had asked after Miss Payne, but he scorned the whole basement.

'Miss who, sir?'

'Miss Payne, of the millinery department.'

'A tall young lady, sir?'

'Yes.'

'With chestnut hair?'

'Now you have me,' he lied.

'I fancy I know who you mean, sir; and now I come to think of it, I don't think she has.'

The waitress spoke in an apologetic tone, and looked at the clock with an apologetic look. She was no fool, that waitress.

'Thank you.'

As he left the room Albert Shawn entered by the other door, and, perceiving nobody but the waitress, kissed the waitress, and was kissed by her heartily.

Hugo's deportment was debonnair, but his heart had seriously sunk. Just as he had before been quite sure that Camilla would come as usual, now he was quite sure that she would not come as usual. Ever since he had learnt from Ravengar that Tudor had been ignorant of Ravengar's presence in the flat, and that Ravengar had had to 'dispose of' the housekeeper, a horrid suspicion had lurked at the back of his mind, and now this suspicion sprang out upon his hopes of Camilla's arrival, and fairly strangled them. And the suspicion was that Camilla had misjudged Francis Tudor, that his intentions had throughout been perfectly honourable, and that on her return to the flat he had quickly convinced Camilla of this.

In which case, where did he, Hugo, come in?

As for the terms of the note, he perceived that he had interpreted them in a particular way because he wished to interpret them in a particular way.

He ascended in the direction of Department 42. Perhaps, after all, she had escaped his vigilance, and was at her duties.

On the way thither he was accosted by a manager.

'Mr. Hugo.'

'Well, Banbury?'

'I telephoned to New Scotland Yard, but they refused any information. However, I've got a pair from the nearest police-station. I shall order our blacksmiths to make a dozen pairs to pattern. They will be in next month's catalogue.'

'I congratulate you, Banbury.'

And he passed on. The early-rising customers were beginning to invade the galleries, the cashiers in their confessional-boxes were settling themselves in their seats, faultless shopwalkers were giving a final hitch to their lovely collars, and the rank-and-file were preparing to receive cavalry. The vast machine had started, slowly and deliberately, as an express engine starts. And already the heat, as yesterday, was formidable. But *she* would not suffer to-day; she was not in Department 42.

He went further and further, aimlessly penetrating to the very heart of the jungle of departments. He had glimpses of departments that he had not seen for weeks. At length he came to the verdant and delicious Flower Department (hot-house branch), and by chance he caught a word which brought him to a standstill.

'What's that?' he asked sharply, of a salesman in white.

'Order for orange-blossom, sir. A single sprig only. Rather a curious order, sir.'

'You can supply it?'

'Without doubt, sir.'

'Who is the customer?'

'Mr. Francis Tudor,' replied the salesman, looking at a paper. 'No. 7, the Flats.'

'Ah yes,' he said; and thought: 'My life is over.'

He gazed with unseeing eyes into the green and shady recesses of the palmarium, where water trickled and tinkled.

What was the power, the influence, the lever, which Francis Tudor was using to induce Camilla to marry him—him whom, on her own statement, she did not love? And could Louis Ravengar be in earnest, after all, with his savage threats?

CHAPTER IX

'WHICH?'

'And when I decide, the thing is as good as done.' Those proud, vain words of his, spoken to Louis Ravengar with all the arrogance of a man who had never met Fate like a lion in the path, often recurred to Hugo's mind during the next few weeks. And their futility exasperated him. He had decided to win Camilla, and therefore Camilla was as good as won! Only, she had been married on the very morning of those boastful words by license at a registry-office to Francis Tudor. The strange admixture of orange-blossom and registry-office was not the only strange thing about the wedding. It was clear, for example, that Tudor must have arranged the preliminaries of the ceremony before the bride's consent had been obtained—unless, indeed, Camilla had garbled the truth to Hugo on the previous night; and Hugo did not believe this to be possible.

Albert Shawn had brought the news hour by hour to Hugo.

After the wedding, the pair drove to Mr. Tudor's flat, where Senior Polycarp paid them a brief visit.

Then Hugo received by messenger a note from Tudor formally regretting that his wife had left her employment without due notice, and enclosing a cheque for the amount of a month's wages in lieu thereof.

And then Mr. and Mrs. Tudor had departed for Paris by the two-twenty Folkstone-Boulogne service from Charing Cross. And the gorgeous flat was shut up.

Albert Shawn had respectfully inquired whether there remained anything else to be done in the affair, far more mysterious to Albert than it was even to Hugo.

'No,' Hugo had said shortly.

He was Hugo, with extraordinary resources at hand, but a quite ordinary circumstance, such as ten minutes spent in a registry-office, will sometimes outweigh all the resources in the world when the success of a scheme hangs in the balance.

What could he do, in London or in Paris, civilized and police-ridden cities?

Civilization left him but one thing to do—to acknowledge his defeat, and to mourn the incomparable beauty and the distinguished spirit which had escaped his passionate grasp. And to this acknowledgment and this mourning he was reduced, feeling that he was no longer Hugo.

It was perhaps natural, however, that his employés should have been made to feel that he was more Hugo than ever. For a month he worked as he had never worked before, and three thousand five hundred people, perspiring under his glance and under the sun of a London August, knew exactly the reason why. The intense dramatic and sentimental interest surrounding Camilla Payne's disappearance from Department 42 was the sole thing which atoned to the legionaries for the inconvenience of Hugo's mistimed activity.

Then suddenly he fell limp; he perceived the uselessness of this attempt to forget in Sloane Street, and he decided to try the banks of a certain trout-stream on Dartmoor. He knew that with all the sun-glare of that season, and the water doubtless running a great deal too fine, he would be as likely to catch trout on Dartmoor as on the Thames Embankment; but he determined to go, and he announced his determination, and the entire personnel, from the managers to the sweepers, murmured privily, 'Thank Heaven!'

The moment came for the illustrious departure. His electric coupé stood at his private door, and his own luggage and Simon Shawn's luggage—for Simon never entrusted his master to other hands—lay on the roof of the coupé. Simon, anxiously looking at his watch, chatted with the driver. Hugo had been stopped on emerging from the lift by the chief accountant concerning some technical question. At length he came out into the street.

'Shaving it close, aren't we, Simon?' he remarked, and sprang into the vehicle, and Simon banged the door and sprang on to the box, and they seemed to be actually off, much to the relief of Simon, who wanted a holiday badly.

But they were not actually off. At that very instant, as the driver pulled his lever, Albert Shawn came frantically into the scene from somewhere, and signalled the driver to wait. Simon cursed his brother.

'Mr. Hugo,' Albert whispered, as he put his head into the coupé.

'Well, my lad?'

'I suppose you've heard? They've turned up again at the flat. Yes, this morning.'

'Who have turned up again?'

'That's the point, sir. Some of 'em. And there's been a funeral ordered.'

'A funeral? Whose funeral? From *us*?

'Yes, sir; but whose—that's another point. You see, I've just run along to let you know how far I've got. Not that you gave me any instructions. But when I heard of a funeral—'

'Is it a man's or a woman's?' Hugo demanded, thinking to himself: 'I must keep calm. I must keep calm.'

'Don't know, sir.'

'But surely the order-book—'

'No order for coffin, sir. Merely the cortège; day after to-morrow; parties making their own arrangements at cemetery. Brompton.'

'And did none of the porters see who arrived at the flat this morning?'

'None of 'em knows enough to be sure, sir.'

'Well,' said Hugo, 'there isn't likely to be a funeral without a coffin, and no porter could be blind to a coffin going upstairs.'

'I can't get wind of any coffin, sir.'

'And that's all you've learnt?'

'That's the hang of it, sir—up to now. But I can wire you to-night or to-morrow, with further particulars.'

Hugo glanced at the carriage-clock in front of him, and thought of the famine of porters at Waterloo Station in August, and invented several other plausible excuses for a resolution which he foresaw that he was about to arrive at.

'You've made me miss my train,' he said, pretending to be annoyed.

'Sorry, sir. Simon, the governor isn't going.'

Simon descended from the box for confirmation, a fratricide in all but deed.

'Have the luggage taken upstairs,' Hugo commanded.

He sat for seven hours in the dome, scarcely moving.

At nine o'clock Albert was announced.

'Coffin just come up, sir,' he said, 'from railway-station.'

But that was the limit of his news.

Within an hour Hugo went to bed. He could not sleep; he had known that he could not sleep. The wild and savage threat of Louis Ravengar, and the question, 'Which?' haunted his brain. At one o'clock in the morning he switched on all the lights, rose out of bed, and walked aimlessly about the chamber. Something, some morbid impulse, prompted him to take up the General Catalogue, which lay next to a priceless copy of the 1603 edition of Florio's 'Montaigne.' There were pages and pages about funerals in the General Catalogue, and forty fine photographic specimens of tombstones and monuments.

'Funerals conducted in town or country.... Cremations and embalmments undertaken.... Special stress is laid on the appearance and efficiency of the attendants, and on the reverent manner in which they perform all their duties.... A shell finished with satin, with robe, etc.... All necessary service.... A hearse (or open car, as preferred) and four horses, three mourning coaches, with two horses each. Coachmen and attendants in mourning, with gloves. Superintendent, £38.... Estimates for cremation on application.... Broken column, in marble, £70. The same, with less carving, £48.' And so on, and so on; and at the top of every page: 'Hugo, Sloane Street, London. Telegraphic address: "Complete, London." Hugo, Sloane Street, London. Telegraphic address: "Complete, London." Hugo —'

Whom was he going to bury the day after to-morrow—he, Hugo, undertaker, with his reverent attendants of appearance guaranteed respectable?

The great catalogue slipped to the floor with a terrible noise, and Simon Shawn sprang out from his lair, and stopped at the sight of his master in pyjamas under the full-blazing electric chandelier.

'All serene,' said Hugo; 'I only dropped a book. Go to sleep. Perhaps we may reach Devonshire to-morrow,' he added kindly.

He sympathized with Simon.

'Yes, sir.'

He thought he would take a stroll on the roof; it might calm his nerves.... Foolishness! How much wiser to take a sedative!

Then he turned to the Montaigne, and after he had glanced at various pages, his eye encountered a sentence in italics: *'Wisdome hath hir excesses, and no lesse need of moderation, than follie.'*

'True,' he murmured.

He dressed, and went out.

CHAPTER X

THE COFFIN

He was in that mental condition, familiar to every genuine man of action, in which, though the mind divides against itself, and there is an apparently even conflict between two impulses, the battle is lost and won before it is fought, and the fight is nothing but a sham fight. He wandered about the roofs; he went as far as the restaurant garden, and turned on all the electric festoons and standards by the secret switch, and sat down solitary at a table before an empty glass which a waiter had forgotten to remove. He extinguished the lights, wandered back to the dome, climbed to the topmost gallery, and saw the moon rising over St. Paul's Cathedral. He said he would go to bed again at once, well knowing that he would not go to bed again at once. He swore that he would conquer the overmastering impulse, well knowing that it would conquer him. He cursed, as men only curse themselves. And then, suddenly, he yielded, gladly, with relief.

He hastened out, and did not pause till he reached the balcony of flat No. 7 in the further quadrangle. He admitted frankly now that the dominant impulse which controlled his mind would force him to enter the flat during that night, by means lawful or unlawful, and he perceived with satisfaction that the great French window of the drawing-room was not quite shut. The blinds, however, had been carefully lowered, and nothing of the interior was revealed save the fact that a light burned within. In the entire quadrangle, round which, tier above tier, hundreds of people were silent in sleep or in vigil, this was the sole illumination. Hugo leaned over the balcony, and tried to pierce the depths of the vast pit below, and those thoughts came to him which come to watchers by night in the presence of sleeping armies, or on the high sea. The eternal and insoluble question troubled and teased him, and would not be put aside. In imagination, he felt the very swish of the planet as it whirled through space with its cargo of pitiful humanity. What, after all, were life, love, ambition, grief, death? What, in the incessant march of suns, could be the value of a few restless specks of vitality clinging with desperation to a minor orb?

And then he fancied he could hear a sound within the flat, and he forgot these transcendental speculations, and for him the secret of the universe lay behind the blinds of Francis Tudor's drawing-room. Yes, he could hear a sound. It was the distant sound of a man talking—loudly, slowly, and distinctly—but too far off for him to catch even one word. He guessed, as he pushed the window a little wider open, and bent his ear to the aperture, that the voice must be in a room beyond the drawing-room. It continued monotonously for a long time, with little breaks at rare intervals; it was rather like a parson reading a sermon in an empty church. Then it ceased. And there were footsteps, which approached the window, and retired. He noticed that the light within the room was being moved, but it cast no human shadow on the blind. The light came finally to a standstill, and then there followed sounds which Hugo could not diagnose—short, regular sounds, broken occasionally by a sharp clash, as of an instrument falling. And when these had come to an end, there were more footsteps—a precise, quick walking to and fro, which continued for ages of time. Lastly, the footsteps receded; something dropped, not heavily, but rather in a manner gently subsiding, and a groan (or was it a moan, a tired suspiration?) wakened in Hugo's spinal column a curious, strange thrill. Then silence, complete, definitive, terrifying.

By merely pushing the window against the blind, he could enter and know the secret of the universe.

'Why am I doing this?' he asked himself, while he pushed the window. 'Why have I done this?' he asked himself, as he stood within the immense and luxurious room.

He gazed round with a swift and timid glance, as a man would who expects to see that which ought not to be seen. To his left was the fireplace, with a magnificent mirror over it. On the mantelpiece burned a movable electric table—lamp, with twin branched lights. He observed the silk-covered cord lying across the mantelpiece and disappearing over the further edge; by the side of the lamp was a screwdriver. Exactly in front of the lamp, on a couple of trestles such as undertakers use, lay an elm coffin, its head towards the mantelpiece. At the opposite end of the room was another fireplace and another mirror, with the result that Hugo saw an endless succession of coffins and corpse-lights, repeated and repeated, till they were lost in a vague crystal blur, and by every pair of corpse-lights was a screwdriver.

He stood moveless, and listened, and could detect no faintest sound. Across the room from the principal window there was a doorway with a heavy portière; not a fold of the portière stirred. To his right, near the other window, was a door—the door by which Camilla had entered that night a month ago; it was shut. His glance searched among the rich confusion of furniture—fauteuils, occasional tables, sofas, statuary, vases, cabinets. He peered into every corner of the silent chamber, and saw nothing that gave a sign of life. He even gazed up guiltily at the decorated ceiling, as though some Freemason's Eye might be scanning him from above.

The coffin reigned in the room; all else was subservient to its massive and sinister presence, and the bright twin-lamps watched over its majesty with dazzling orbs.

Hugo went near the coffin, stepping on tip-toe over the thick-piled rugs, and examined it. There was no name-plate. He looked at himself in the mirror, and again he murmured a question: 'Why am I here?' Then he listened attentively, fearfully. No sound. His hands travelled to the screwdriver on the mantelpiece, and then fifty of his hands picked up fifty screwdrivers. And he listened once more. No sound.

'I must do it. I must,' he thought.

The next moment he was unscrewing the screws in the lid of the coffin, and scarcely had he begun the task when he realized that what he had heard from the balcony was the screwing of these same screws. There were twelve, and some of them were difficult to start, but in due course he had removed them all, and they stood in a row on their heads on the mantelpiece. He listened yet again. No sound. He had only to push the lid of the coffin to the left or to the right, or to lift it up. He spent several seconds in deciding whether he should push or lift, and then at length fifty Hugos lifted bodily the lids of fifty coffins. And after a dreadful hesitation he lowered his gaze and looked.

Yes, it was Camilla! He had known always that it would be Camilla.

The pale repose of death only emphasized the proud and splendid beauty of that head, with its shut eyes, its mouth firmly closed in a faint smile, and its glorious hair surrounded by all the white frippery of the shroud. Here lay the mortal part of the incomparable creature who had been coveted by three men and won by one—for a few brief days' possession. Here lay the repository of Ravengar's secrets, the grave of Hugo's happiness, the dead mate of Tudor's desire. Here lay the eternal woman, symbol of all beauty and all charm, victimized by her own loveliness. For if she had not been lovely, thought Hugo, if the curves of her cheek and her nostrils and the colour of her skin had been ever so slightly different, the world might have contained one widower, one ruined heart, and one murderer the less that night.

He did not doubt, he could not doubt, after Ravengar's threats, that she had been murdered. And yet he was not angry then. He did not feel a great grief. He was conscious of no sensation save a numbed and desolate awe. He had not begun to feel. Ledging the lid crossways on the coffin, he placed his hand gently upon Camilla's brow. It was colder than he had expected, and it had the peculiar hard, inelastic touch of incipient decay—that touch which communicates a shudder even to the most impassive.

'I must go,' he whispered, staring spell-bound at her face.

He was surprised to find drops of moisture falling on the shroud. They were his tears, and yet he had not known that he was crying.

He hid her again beneath the elm plank, and, taking the screws one by one from the mantel-piece, shut her up for ever from any human gaze. And then, nearly collapsing under a nervous tension such as he had never before experienced, he turned to leave the apartment as he had entered it, like a thief. But the mystery of the heavy velvet portière invincibly attracted him. His steps wavered towards it. He fancied he saw something dark protruding under the curtain, and he pulled the curtain aside with a movement almost hysteric. A man lay extended at full length on his chest in the passage beyond—what Hugo had noticed was his boot.

'Tudor!' he exclaimed, kneeling to examine the half-concealed face.

At the same moment a figure came quietly down the passage. Hugo looked up, and saw a sallow-featured man of about thirty-five in a tourist suit, with light beard and hair, and long thin hands.

'What is this?' asked the stranger evenly. 'Who are you?'

'My name is Hugo,' Hugo answered with assurance. 'I was walking along the balconies, as I do sometimes at night, and I heard strange sounds here, and as the window was open I stepped in and found this. Are you a friend of Mr. Tudor's?'

The other bent in his turn, and after examining the prone body said:

'I was. He has no friends now.'

'You mean he is dead?'

'He must have died within the last quarter of an hour or so.'

'And nothing can be done?'

'Nothing can be done with death!'

'I take it you are a doctor?' said Hugo.

'My name is Darcy,' the other replied. 'Besides being Tudor's friend, I was his physician.'

'Yet even for a physician,' Hugo pursued, 'it seems to me that you have been able to decide very quickly that your friend and patient is dead. I have always understood that to say with assurance that death has taken place means a very careful and thorough examination.'

'You are right,' Darcy agreed, stroking his short, bright, silky beard. 'There is only one absolute proof of death.'

'And that is?'

'Putrefaction. Nevertheless, the inquest will show whether or not I have been in error.'

'There will have to be an inquest?'

'Certainly. In such a case as this no doctor in his senses would give his certificate without a post-mortem, and though I am an enthusiast, I am in my senses, Mr. Hugo.'

'An enthusiast?'

'Let me explain. My friend Tudor was suffering from one of the rarest of all maladies—malignant disease of the heart. The text-books will tell you that malignant disease of the heart has probably never been diagnosed. It is a disease of which there are no symptoms, in which the patient generally suffers no pain, and for which there is no treatment. Nevertheless, in my enthusiasm, I have diagnosed in this case that a very considerable extent of the cardiac wall was affected by epithelioma. We shall see. Not long since I condemned Tudor to an early and sudden death—a death which might be hastened by circumstances.'

'Poor chap!' Hugo murmured.

The dead man looked so young, artless, and content.

'Why "poor"?' Darcy turned on him sharply but coldly. 'Is not a sudden death the best? Would you not wish it for yourself, for your friends?'

'Yes,' said Hugo; 'but when one is dead one is dead. That's all I meant.'

'I have heard much of you, Mr. Hugo,' said the other. 'And, if I may be excused a certain bluntness, it is very obvious that, though you say little, you are no ordinary man. Can it be possible that you have lived so long and so fully and are yet capable of pitying the dead? Have you not learnt that it is only *they* who are happy?' He vaguely indicated the corpse. 'If you will be so good as to assist me—'

'Willingly,' said Hugo, who could find nothing else to say. 'I suppose we must call the servants?'

'Why call the servants? To begin with, there is only one here, a somewhat antique housekeeper. Let her sleep. She has been through sufficient to-day. Morning will be time enough for the futile formalities which civilization has invented to protect itself. Night, which is the season of death, should not be disturbed by them.'

'As you think best,' Hugo concurred.

'And now,' Darcy began, in a somewhat relieved tone, when he had finished his task, and the remains of Francis Tudor lay decently covered on a sofa in the drawing-room, that mortuary chamber, 'will you oblige me by coming into the study for a while? I am not in the mood for sleep, and perhaps you are not. And I will admit frankly that I should prefer not to be alone at present. Yes,' he added, with a faint deprecatory smile, 'my theories about death are thoroughly philosophical, but one cannot always act up to one's theories.'

And in the study, at the other end of the flat, far from the relics of humanity, he began to roll cigarettes with marvellous swiftness in his long thin fingers.

Hugo surmised that under his singular and almost glacial calm the man concealed a temperament highly nervous and sensitive.

'You do not inquire about the—the coffin?' said Darcy at length, when they had smoked for a few moments in silence.

As a fact, Hugo had determined that, at no matter what cost to his feelings, he would not be the first to mention the other fatality.

The two men looked at each other, and each blew out a lance of smoke.

'What did she die of?' Hugo demanded curtly.

'You are aware, then, who it is?'

'Naturally, I guessed.'

'Ah! she died of typhoid fever. You knew her?'

'I knew her.'

'Of course; I remember. She was in your employ. Yes,' he sighed; 'she contracted typhoid fever in Paris. It's always more or less endemic there. And what with this hot summer and their water-supply and their drainage, it's been more rife than usual lately. Tudor called me in at once. I am qualified both in England and France, but I practise in Paris. It was a fairly ordinary case, except that she suffered from severe and persistent headaches at the beginning. But in typhoid the danger is seldom in the fever; it is in the complications. She had a hæmorrhage. I—I failed. A hæmorrhage in typhoid is not necessarily fatal, but it often proves so. She died from exhaustion.'

'I thought,' said Hugo, in a low, unnatural voice, 'that typhoid marked the patient—spots on the face.'

'Not invariably. Oh no; but why do you say that?'

'I only meant that I hope her face was not marked.'

'It was not. You mean that you hope her face was not marked because she was so beautiful?'

'Exactly,' said Hugo. 'And so Tudor brought the body over to England for burial?'

'Yes; he insisted on that. And he insisted on my coming with him. I could not refuse.'

'And now he, too, is gone! Tell me, was he expecting it—his own death?'

Darcy lighted another cigarette.

'Who can say?' he observed to the ceiling. 'Who can say what premonitions such a man may not have had?'

'I heard talking before I came into the flat from the balcony,' said Hugo abruptly. 'It went on for a long time. Was it you and he?'

'No,' the doctor replied; 'I was in here, writing.' He pointed to some papers on a desk. 'I did not even hear him fall.'

'Yet you heard me?'

'No, I didn't. I was just coming to find out what Tudor was doing when I saw you.'

'It is curious that I heard talking, and walking about, too.'

'Possibly he was talking to himself. Did you hear two voices?'

'Perhaps I heard only one.'

'Then no doubt he was talking to himself. You won't be surprised to learn that he had been in an excessively emotional condition all day.... It is all very sad. Only a month ago, and Tudor was—but what am I saying? Who knows what perils and misfortunes he—they—may not have escaped? For my part, I envy—yes, I envy Tudor.'

'But not her? You do not envy her? In your quality of philosophy, you regret *her* death?'

'Do not ask me to be consistent,' said the philosopher, after a long pause.

Hugo rose and approached Darcy.

'Are you acquainted with a man named Louis Ravengar?' he demanded in a rather loud tone.

The doctor scanned his face.

'I have heard Tudor mention the name, but I do not know him.'

'And upon my soul I believe you,' cried Hugo. 'Nevertheless—'

'Nevertheless what?'

Darcy seemed startled. Hugo's strange outburst was indeed startling.

'Oh, nothing!' Hugo muttered. 'Nothing.' He walked to the window, which looked out on Blair Street. The first heralds of the dawn were in the eastern sky, and the moon overhead was paling. 'It will be daylight in a minute,' he said. 'I must go. Come with me first to the drawing-room, will you?'

And they passed together along the passage to the drawing-room, where the electric lamp was still keeping watch. Hugo stood by the side of the coffin.

'What is it?' Darcy quietly asked.

'Have you ever been in love?' Hugo questioned him.

'Yes,' said Darcy.

'Then I will tell you. You will understand. I must tell someone. I loved her.'

He touched the elm-wood gently, and hurried out of the room by the French window.

Four days later Mr. Senior Polycarp called on Hugo in his central office.

In the meantime the inquest had proved the correctness of Mr. Darcy's diagnosis. Francis Tudor was buried, and Francis Tudor's wife was buried. Hugo, who had accompanied the funerals disguised as one of his own 'respectful attendants,' saw scarcely anyone. He had to recover the command of his own soul, and to adopt some definite attitude towards the army of suspicions which naturally had assailed him. Could he believe Darcy? He decided that he could, and that he must. Darcy had inspired him with confidence, and there was no doubt that the man had an extensive practice in Paris, and was well known at the British Embassy. Camilla, then, had really died of typhoid fever on her honeymoon, and hence Ravengar had not murderously compassed her death. And people did die of typhoid fever, and people did die on their honeymoons.

Either Ravengar's threats had been idle, or Fate had mercifully robbed him of the opportunity to execute them. Hugo remembered that he had begun by regarding the threats as idle, and that it was only later, in presence of Camilla's corpse, that he had thought otherwise of them. So he drove back the army of suspicions, and settled down to accustom himself to the eternal companionship of a profound and irremediable grief.

Then it was that Polycarp called.

'I come to you,' said the white-moustached solicitor, 'on behalf of my late client, Mr. Tudor. He made his will after his marriage, and before starting for Paris, and it contains a peculiar clause. Mr. Tudor had the flat on a three years' agreement, renewable at his option for a further period of two years. Over two years of the three are expired.'

'That is so,' said Hugo. 'You want to get rid of the tenancy at once? Well, I don't mind. I can easily—'

'No,' Polycarp interrupted him, 'I wish to give notice of renewal. The will provides that if the testator should die within two months of the date of it the flat shall be sealed up exactly as it stands for twelve months after his death, and that the estate shall be held by me, as executor and trustee, for that period, and then dealt with according to instructions deposited in the testator's private safe in the vault which I rent from you in your Safe Deposit.'

'But—'

'I have just sealed up the flat—doors, windows, ventilators, everything.'

'Mr. Polycarp, this is impossible.'

'Not at all. It is done.'

'But the reason?'

'I know no more than yourself. As executor, I have carried out the terms of the will. I thought that you, as landlord, were entitled to the information which I have given you.'

'As landlord,' said Hugo, 'I object. And I shall demand entrance.'

'On what ground?'

'Under the clause which in all tenancy agreements gives the landlord the right to enter at reasonable times in order to inspect the condition of the premises,' Hugo answered defiantly to the lawyer.

'I had considered that. But I shall dispute the right. You may bring an action. What then? No court will give you leave to force an entrance. An Englishman's furnished flat, just as much as his house, is his castle. I could certainly keep you out for a year.'

'And may I ask why you are so anxious to keep me out, Mr. Polycarp?'

'I am anxious merely to fulfil my duties. May I ask why you are so anxious to get in? Why do you want to thwart the wishes of a dead man?'

'I could not permit that mystery to remain for a whole year in the very middle of my block of flats.'

'What mystery?' Polycarp suavely inquired.

During this brief conversation all Hugo's suspicions had hurriedly returned, and he had examined them anew and more favourably. Polycarp? Was it not curious that Polycarp should be acting for both Ravengar and Tudor?... Darcy? Were there not very strange features in the behaviour of this English doctor who preferred to practise in Paris?... And the hæmorrhage? And, lastly, this monstrous, unaccountable, inexplicable shutting-up of the flat?

He felt already that those empty rooms, dark, silent, sealed, guarding in some recess he knew not what dreadful secret, were getting on his nerves. And was he to suffer for a year?

'Come, Mr. Hugo,' said Polycarp; 'I may count on your goodwill?'

'I don't know,' Hugo replied—'I don't know.'

PART II

THE PHONOGRAPH

CHAPTER XI

SALE

Strange sights are to be seen in London.

At five minutes to nine a.m. on the first day of the year seven vast crowds stood before the seven principal entrances to Hugo's; seven crowds of immortal souls enclosed in the bodies of women. They meant to begin the year well by an honest attempt to get something for nothing. It was a cold, dank, raw, and formidable morning; Hugo's tessellated pavements were covered with moisture, and, moreover, day had not yet conquered night. But the seven crowds, growing larger each moment, recked nothing of these inconveniences. They waited stolidly, silently, in a suppressed and dangerous fever, as besiegers await the signal for an attack. Between the various entrances, on the three façades of the establishment, ran the long lines of windows dressed with all the materials for happiness, and behind these ramparts of materials could be glimpsed Hugo's assistants moving about in anxious expectation under the electric lights, which burned red in the foggy gloom. Over every portal was a purple warning: 'Beware of pickpockets, male and female.' No possible male pickpockets, however, were visible to the eye; perhaps they were disguised as ladies. The seven crowds wedged themselves closer and closer, clutched tighter and tighter their purses, and stared at the golden commissionaires through the glass doors with a glance more and more ferocious. Then suddenly something went off with a boom; it was the first stroke of the great Hugo clock under the dome. Six pairs of double doors opened simultaneously, six pairs of golden commissionaires were overthrown like ninepins, and in a fraction of time six companies of determined and remorseless women had swept like Prussian cavalry into the interior of the doomed edifice.

But the seventh crowd was left on the pavement, for the seventh pair of doors had not opened. And this was the more extraordinary in that the seventh crowd was the largest crowd, and stood before the entrance nearest to the principal scene of the day's operations. Instantly the world became aware that Hugo's management was less perfect than usual, and people recalled incidents in his business during the previous four months which had not been to his credit. The seventh crowd was staggered, furious, and homicidal. If glances could have killed the impassive pair of golden commissionaires behind the seventh portal, they would certainly have fallen down dead. If the glass of the seventh portal had not been set in small squares of immense thickness, it would have been shattered to bits, and the stronghold forced. Many women cried out that justice had come to an end in England, for was it not an elementary principle of justice that all doors should open together? A few women, more practical, and near the edge of the enraged horde, slipped away to other entrances. One woman fainted, but she was held upright by the press, and as no one paid the slightest attention to her she rapidly came to. Then at length a tall gentleman in a beautiful frock-coat was seen to be expostulating sternly with the seventh pair of golden commissionaires; the recalcitrant doors flew open, and the beautiful frock-coat was hurled violently against a marble pillar for its pains. Just as the seventh regiment was disappearing to join in the sack and loot, a young and pretty girl drove up in a hansom, threw the driver a shilling (which the driver contemplated with a scorn too deep for words), and joined the tail of the regiment.

'I knew I should do it,' she said to herself, 'and Alb said I shouldn't.'

In another moment Hugo's was a raging sea of petticoats. In half an hour the doors had to be shut and locked, and new crowds formed on the tessellated pavements; Hugo's was full.

Hugo's was full!

For three days past Hugo had bought whole pages of every daily paper in London, in order to break gently to the public the tremendous fact that his annual sale would commence on New Year's Day, and the still more tremendous fact that it would close on the third of January. There are only three genuine annual sales in the Metropolis. One is Hugo's, another happens in Tottenham Court Road, and the third—but why disclose the situation of the third, since all persons from Putney to Peckham Rise who are worthy to know it, know it? Hugo's was naturally the greatest, the largest, the most exciting, the most marvellous, the most powerful in its appeal to the most powerful of human instincts—the instinct to get half a crown's worth of value for two shillings. In earlier years Hugo had made his annual sale prodigious and incredible, with no thought of profit, merely for the pleasure of the affair. But he found that the more he offered to the public the more he received from them, and that it was practically impossible to lose money by giving things away. This is, of course, a fundamental axiom of commerce. And now Hugo's annual sale was to be more astonishing than ever; some said that he meant at any cost to efface the memory of those discreditable incidents before mentioned. Decidedly, many of the advertised bargains were remarkable in the highest degree. There was, for example, the 'fine silvered fox-stole, with real brush at each end,' at a guinea. Every woman who can tell a silvered fox-stole from a cock's-feather boa is aware that a silvered fox-stole simply cannot be sold for a guinea. Yet Hugo had announced that he would sell two thousand of them at that price, not to mention muffs to match at the same figure. And there was the famous 'Incroyable' corset, white coutille, with wide belted band round hips, double belt to buckle at sides, cut low—' Enough! Further indiscretions of description are not necessary to show that eighteen and nine is the lowest price at which a reasonable creature could hope to obtain the 'Incroyable' corset. But Hugo's price was twelve and eleven. And the whole-page advertisements were a solid blazing mass of such jewels.

The young and pretty girl who had known that she would 'do it' hastened with assured steps, and as quickly as the jostling multitudes would allow, to the fur department. She was in pursuit of one of the silvered fox-stoles with real brush at each end. She had her husband's permission—nay, his command—to purchase a silvered fox-stole at a guinea—if she could. On the way to her goal she encountered by chance Simon Shawn, and it occurred that a temporary block compelled her to halt before him. The two gazed at each other, and Simon looked away, flushing. It was plain that, though acquainted, they were not on speaking terms. The fact was, that their silence covered a domestic drama—a drama which had arisen as the consequence of a great human truth—namely, that even detectives will marry.

It will be remembered that on a certain morning in July, after Hugo had finished pasting a notice on a mirror in one of the common rooms, in the presence of a pink-aproned waitress, Albert Shawn entered, and kissed the pink-aproned waitress. So far as possible, whom Albert Shawn kissed he married, and he had married the waitress just the week before Christmas, and this was she. Simon had objected sternly to the *mésalliance*. It seemed shocking to Simon that a rising detective should marry a girl who waited on shop-girls. Hence the drama. Hugo had positively refused to allow an open quarrel between the brothers, because of its inconvenience to himself, but he could not prevent a quarrel between Simon and Lily—such was her name. They met now for the first time since the marriage, and Lily's demeanour may be imagined. She gazed through Simon as though he did not exist, and passed magnificently onwards as soon as the throng permitted. She was Mrs. Albert Shawn, as neat as ninepence, as smart and pert as a French maid out for the day. She drove in hansoms, and she had a five-pound note in her pocket.

Albert had been granted two weeks' vacation for his honeymoon, and he ought to have resumed his duties of detection that morning. The honeymoon, however, had lasted only nine days, and the remaining five days of the period had been spent by him in some secret affair of his own, an affair which had ended in an accident to his left foot, so that he could not walk. The consequence was that, on this day of all days, Hugo's was deprived of his services. Lily was, perhaps, not altogether sorry for the catastrophe which kept him a prisoner in the nest-like home in Radipole Road, for it had resulted in this excursion of hers to the sale. Albert had bidden her to go to buy a stole and other things, to keep her eyes open, and to report to Hugo in person if she observed anything queer. He had even given her a pass which would ensure her immediate admittance to any of Hugo's private lairs. Therefore, Lily felt extremely important, extremely like a detective's wife. She knew that Albert trusted her, and she was very proud that she had not asked him any questions concerning a matter exasperatingly mysterious. Albert had taught her that a detective's wife should crucify curiosity.

She fought her way to a counter in the fur department.

'The guinea stoles?' she inquired from a shopwalker.

'I—I beg pardon, miss,' said the shopwalker.

'Madam,' Lily corrected him. 'I want one of those silvered fox-stoles advertised at a guinea.'

'You'll probably find them over there, madam,' said the shopwalker, pointing.

'Aren't you sure?' she asked tartly. 'I don't want to struggle across there and then find they're somewhere else.'

The shopwalker turned his back on her.

'Well, I never!' she exclaimed to herself, and decided that Albert should avenge her.

Then, behind the counter, she saw a girl whom she used to serve with a glass of milk every morning.

'Oh, Miss Lawton,' she cried, as an equal to an equal, 'can you tell me where the stoles are to be found?'

'Probably over there, Mrs. Shawn,' said Miss Lawton kindly, nodding the greeting she had no time to utter.

So Lily got away from the counter, plunged into a chartless sea of customers, and eventually emerged in the quarter which had been indicated.

'All sold out, miss!'

Such was the blunt answer to her demand for a silvered fox-stole.

'Don't talk to me like that!' said Mrs. Albert Shawn. 'It isn't above half-past nine on the first morning of the sale, and you advertised two thousand of them.'

'Sorry, miss. All sold out,' repeated the second shopwalker.

'I shall report this to Mr. Hugo. Do you know who I am? I'm—'

And the second shopwalker also turned his back.

Could these things be happening at Hugo's, at Hugo's, so famous for the courtesy, the long patience, the indestructible politeness of its well-paid employés? And could Hugo have descended to the trickeries of the eleven-pence-halfpenny draper, who proclaimed non-existent bargains to lure the unwary into his shop? Lily might have wondered if she was not dreaming, but she was far too practical ever to be in the least doubt as to whether she was asleep or awake. And now she perceived that scores of angry women about her were equally disappointed by the disgraceful absence of those stoles. The department, misty, stuffy, and noisy, had the air of being the scene of an insurrection. One lady was informing the public generally that she had demanded a guinea stole at three minutes past nine, and had been put off with a monstrous excuse. And then a newspaper reporter appeared, and began to take notes. The din increased, though shopwalkers said less and less, and the chances seemed in favour of the insurrection becoming a riot. Other admirable bargains in furs were indubitably to be had—muffs, for example—and the cashiers were busy; but nothing could atone for the famine of stoles.

Lily had a suspicion that Albert would have wished her to report these singular circumstances to Hugo at once. But she dismissed the suspicion, because she passionately desired an 'Incroyable' corset at twelve and eleven, and she feared lest the corsets might have vanished as strangely as the stoles. In ten minutes, breathless, she had reached the corset department, demanded an 'Incroyable' of the correct size, and bought it. There was no dissatisfaction in the corset department.

'Shall we send it, miss?'

'Madam,' said Lily proudly. 'No, I'll take it.'

'Yes, madam.'

At the cash desk (No. 56) she had to wait her turn in a disorderly queue before she could tender the bill and her five-pound note. Customers pressed round her on all sides as she put down the note and peered through the wire network into the interior of the desk.

'Next, please,' said the cashier sharply, after a moment.

'My change,' demanded Lily.

'You have had it, madam.'

'Oh,' said Lily, 'I have had it, have I? Now, none of your nonsense, young man! Do you know who I am? I'm Mrs. Albert Shawn.'

'Mr. Randall,' the cashier called out coldly, and a grave and gigantic shopwalker appeared who knew not the name of Albert Shawn, and who firmly told Mrs. Shawn that if she wished to make a complaint she must make it at the Central Inquiry Office, ground-floor, Department 1A.

Lily had been brazenly robbed at Hugo's by an employé of Hugo! She was elbowed away by other women apparently anxious to be robbed. She wanted to cry, but suddenly remembering her identity, and her pass to the presence of Hugo, she threw up her head and marched off through the crowds.

She had not proceeded twenty yards before she was stopped by a group of persons round a policeman—a policeman obviously called in from Sloane Street. A stout woman of lady-like appearance had been arrested on a charge of attempted pocket-picking. An accusatory shopwalker charged her, and she replied warmly that she was Lady Brice (*née* Kentucky-Webster), the American wife of the well-known philanthropist, and that her carriage was waiting outside. The policeman and the shopwalker smiled. It was so easy to be the wife of a well-known philanthropist, and in these days all the best pickpockets had their carriages waiting outside.

'I know this lady by sight,' said Lily. 'She visited the common-rooms last year to see the arrangements, with Mr. Hugo, and he called her Lady Brice, and I can tell you he'll be very angry with you.'

'And who are *you*, my young friend?' said the policeman sceptically, and threateningly.

'I'm—'

The formula proved useless. Lady Brice (*née* Kentucky-Webster) was led off in all her vast speechless, outraged impeccability, and poor little Lily was glad to escape with her freedom and the memory of Lady Brice's grateful bow.

She ran, gliding in and out between the knots of visitors, until she was stopped by a pair of doors being suddenly shut and fastened in her face. The reason for the obstruction was plain. Those doors admitted to the blouse department, and the blouse department, as Lily could see through the diamond panes, was a surging sea of bargain-hunters, amid which shopwalkers stood up like light-houses, while the girls behind the counters trembled in fear of being washed away. Discipline, order, management, had ceased to exist at Hugo's.

Mrs. Shawn turned to seek another route, but already dozens of women were upon her, and she could not retire. The crowd of candidates for admission to the blouse department swelled till it filled the gallery between that department and its neighbour. Then someone cried out for air, and someone else protested that the doors at the other end of the short gallery had also been shut. Lily, whose manifold misfortunes had not quenched her interest in the 'Incroyable' corset, opened her parcel, and found that the corset was not an 'Incroyable' at all, but an inferior substitute, with no proper belted band, and of a shape to startle even a Brighton bathing-woman! The change must have been effected by the assistant in making up the parcel.

'Well!'

She could say no more, and think no more, than this 'Well!'

And, moreover, the condition of the packed gallery soon caused her to forget even the final swindle of the corset. The air had rapidly become exhausted. Women clutched at each other; women rapped frenziedly against the heavy, glazed doors; women screamed. It was the Black Hole of Calcutta over again, and yet no one in the blouse department seemed to notice the signals of distress. Lily felt the perspiration on her brow and chin, and then she knew that she, too, must scream and clutch; and she cried out, and the pressure which forced her against the door grew more and more terrible.... She had dropped the corset.... She murmured feebly 'Alb—'.... She began to dream queer dreams and to see strange lights.... And then something gave way with a crash, and she fell forward, and regiments of horses trampled over her, and at last all living things receded from her, and she was in the midst of a great silence. And then even the silence was gone, and there was nothing.

So ended the first part of Lily's adventures at Hugo's infamous annual sale.

When she recovered perfect consciousness, she was in the dome. She knew it was the dome because Albert had once, at her urgent request, taken her surreptitiously to see it. Simon was standing over her, as sympathetic as the most exigent sister-in-law could wish, and the great Shawn family feud had expired.

In two minutes she was her intensely practical self again. In five minutes she had acquainted Simon with all her experiences; they were but the complement of what he himself had witnessed.

The sense of a mysterious calamity over-hanging Hugo's, and the sense of the shame which had already disgraced Hugo's, pressed heavily on both of them. They knew that only one man could retrieve what had been lost and avert irreparable disaster. Their faith in that man was undiminished, and Simon at least was sure that he had been victimized by some immense conspiracy.

'Why don't you find Mr. Hugo?' Lily demanded.

'I've looked everywhere. A letter was brought up to him about an hour ago, and he went off instantly.'

'And where's the letter?'

'I expect it's in that drawer, where he throws all his private letters,' said Simon, pointing to a drawer in the big writing-table on the opposite side of the room from the piano.

'Is it locked—the drawer?'

'No.'

'Then open it.'

'It's the governor's private drawer,' said Simon. 'I've never—'

'Stuff!' Lily exclaimed, and she opened the drawer and drew out the topmost letter.

It was on blue paper.

'Yes, that's it,' said Simon. 'The envelope was blue, I remember.'

'He must be in the Safe Deposit,' said Lily, perusing the letter with flying glance.

And Simon, at length sufficiently emboldened, seized the letter and read:

'SIR,

'Mr. Polycarp has just been here, and accidentally left behind him keys of his vault, including safe of late Mr. Francis Tudor, etc. In these peculiar circumstances I shall be glad to know what I am to do.

'Yours respectfully,

'H. BROWN,

'Head Guardian,

'Hugo's Safe Deposit.'

'What on earth can Brown be thinking about?' muttered Simon. 'Hadn't he got enough gumption to send a messenger after Mr. Polycarp, without troubling the governor? He'll catch it.'

'Never mind that,' said Lily sharply. 'Run down to the Safe Deposit. Run, Simon.'

It was as though a delay of minutes might mean ruin. Who could say what was even then happening in the disorganized and masterless departments?

CHAPTER XII

SAFE DEPOSIT

The Safe Deposit at Hugo's was perhaps the most wonderful of all the departments. Until Hugo thought of it, and paid a trinity of European experts to design and devise it, there had existed no such thing as an absolutely impregnable asylum for valuables. In Dakota a strong-room alleged to be impregnable had been approached underground, tunnelled, mined, and emptied by thieves with imagination. In the North of England a safe, which its inventor had defied the whole universe of crime to open, had been rifled by the aid of so simple a dodge as duplicate keys. Even in Tottenham Court Road a couple of ingenious persons had burnt a hole in a guaranteed safe by means of common gas at three and threepence per thousand cubic feet. These surprises could not occur at Hugo's. His Safe Deposit really was what it pretended to be. All contingencies were provided for. It was the final retort of virtue to vice.

You approached it by a door of quite ordinary appearance (no one cares to be seen leaving what is obviously a safe deposit), and you signed your name before entering a lift. You descended forty feet below the surface of the earth, gave a password on emerging from the lift, traversed a corridor, and at length stood in front of the sole entrance to the Safe Deposit. A guardian, when you had signed your name again, unlocked three unpickable, incombustible, and gunpowder-proof locks in a massive steel door, and you were admitted, assuming always that the hour was between nine and six. Out of hours and on Saturday after-noons and on Sundays a time-lock rendered it utterly impossible for any person whatever to turn any key in the Safe Deposit. Once the lock was set, Hugo himself could not have entered, not even to save the British Empire from instant destruction, until the time-lock had run its course.

You found yourself in an electrically lighted world of passages built in flashing steel, with floors of steel and ceilings of steel—a world where the temperature was always 65°. Every passage was separated from every other passage by steel grilles, and at intervals uniformed and gigantic officials wandered about with impassive, haughty faces—faces that indicated a sublime confidence in the safety of the multifarious riches committed to their care. You might have guessed yourself in the fell grip of the Inquisition. As a fact, you were in something far more fell. You were in a vast chamber of steel, and that chamber was itself enclosed on all sides by three feet of solid concrete. No thief could tunnel or mine you without first getting through the District Railway on the one hand, or the main drainage system of London on the other. No thief could rifle you by means of duplicate keys, for no vault and no safe could be opened except in the presence of the head guardian, who possessed a key without which the renter's key was useless. No tricks could be played with the gas, because there was no gas, and the electric light could only be turned off or on from the top of the lift-well.

Now, it was a singular thing that when Simon Shawn, having proved his identity and his mission at the lift, arrived at the entrance to the Safe Deposit, he discovered the great steel door ajar, and no door-guardian in the leather chair where a door-guardian always sat. This condition of affairs did not affect the essential impregnability of any individual vault or safe, but, nevertheless, it was singular.

Simon walked straight in.

'There's no one at the door,' he said to the patrol, whom he met in the main passage. 'I want to see Mr. Hugo at once. He's down here somewhere, or he's been here.'

'Yes, Mr. Shawn,' said the patrol politely; 'I did see Mr. Hugo here about an hour or so ago. I'll ask Mr. Brown. Will you step into the waiting-room?'

Half-way along the main corridor was a large room, whose steel walls were masked by tapestries, where renters could examine their treasures on marble tables. It was empty when Simon went in. The patrol carefully closed the door on him, and then in a moment came back to say that Mr. Brown was not in his office, and had probably gone out to lunch, the hour being noon.

'Where did you see Mr. Hugo?' Simon asked, hurrying out of the room in a state of considerable agitation.

'I saw him just here, sir,' said the patrol, turning down a short side corridor—the grille was unfastened—and stopping before a door numbered thirty-nine. 'He was talking to Mr. Brown, and the door of the vault was open.'

'That must be Mr. Polycarp's vault,' Simon observed; and then he started, and put his ear against the door. 'Listen!' he exclaimed to the patrol. 'Can't you hear anything inside?'

And the patrol also put his ear to the steel face of the door.

'I seem to hear a faint knocking, but it's that faint as you scarcely *can* hear it. There! it's stopped.'

'He is inside,' Shawn whispered.

'Who's inside?'

'Mr. Hugo.'

'It's God help him, then,' said the patrol, 'if he's there long. There's no ventilation, Mr. Shawn. We'd better telephone for Mr. Polycarp. The other key will be in the key-safe. I can get it. But how do you make out, sir, that Mr. Hugo can be in there? The vault could only be locked by Mr. Polycarp and Mr. Brown together, and surely they couldn't both—'

'Mr. Polycarp left his keys behind by accident. He had gone before Mr. Hugo came down.'

'There's been no Mr. Polycarp here this morning,' said the patrol a minute later. 'I've looked at the signature-book. I thought it was queer I hadn't seen him. And, what's more, that isn't Mr. Polycarp's vault at all. Mr. Polycarp's vault is No. 37. This vault has been empty for several weeks.'

'Then you have both the keys?' Simon demanded quickly.

'No, sir. It's very strange. There's only one key of No. 39 in the key-safe, and it's the renter's key.'

'Then Mr. Brown must have the other.'

'I expect so. But he ought not to have. It's against rules,' said the patrol. 'I know where he takes his lunch. I'll send for him.'

Simon put his ear again to the face of the door. The faint knocking had ceased, but after a few seconds it recommenced.

'And suppose you don't find Mr. Brown?' he queried, still listening.

'Then that vault can't be opened. But never you fear, Mr. Shawn. I'll have him here in three minutes. It's funny as he should have left anybody in there by accident—and Mr. Hugo of all people in this blessed world....'

The patrol's accents died away as he passed down the main corridor.

Within the next half-hour Simon, who had the rare virtue of being honest with himself, was freely admitting, in the privacy of his own mind, that the crisis had got beyond his power to grapple with it, and he had begun to fear complications more dreadful than he dared to put into words. For the patrol had failed to find Mr. Brown. Mr. Brown, head guardian of the Safe Deposit, had disappeared. Nor was this all. A renter had come to take his belongings from a safe in the third side-passage on the left, and the sub-guardian imprisoned in that passage could not open the grille between it and the main corridor. He had his key, but the key would not turn in the glittering lock. The renter, too impatient to wait, had departed very angrily at this excess of safety. Then it was gradually discovered that every sub-guardian in every side-passage was similarly imprisoned. Not a key in the entire place would turn. The patrol rushed to the main door. The three keys had clearly been turned while the door was opened, and the shot bolts prevented the door from closing. This explained why the door was ajar, but it did not explain the absence of the doorkeeper, who had apparently followed in the footsteps of his chief, Mr. Brown.

'The time-lock! Someone must have set it!' cried the patrol to Shawn, and the two hastened to the other end of the main corridor, where the dial of the machine glistened under an electric lamp.

And all the sub-guardians stirred and grumbled in their beautiful bright cages like wrathful lions. No such scene had ever been known in that Safe Deposit or any other safe deposit before.

The patrol was right. The dial of the time-lock showed that it had been set against every lock, great and small, in the Safe Deposit, until nine a.m. the next day.

'It's all up!' the patrol said solemnly.

'Do you mean to say nothing can be done to open that vault till nine to-morrow?' Simon demanded in despair.

'Nothing. The blooming Czar couldn't manage it with all his Cossacks! No, nor Bobs either! This is a Safe Deposit, this is, and if Mr. Hugo is in that vault, it's Mr. Hugo as knows it's a Safe Deposit by now.'

A brief silence ensued, and then Simon said:

'We must telephone to the police. There's a telephone in the waiting-room, isn't there?'

The patrol admitted that there was, but his manner hinted a low opinion of the utility of the police. He stood mute while Simon Shawn told the telephone receiver what had occurred in the bowels of the earth beneath Hugo's.

'Wait a minute,' said the telephone, and then, after a pause: 'Are you there? I'm Inspector Winter.'

'That's him as has charge of all the strong-room cases,' the patrol interjected to Simon.

'I've got Mr. Jack Galpin here, as it happens,' said the telephone.

'Mr. Jack Galpin?' Simon questioned.

'He's just done eighteen months for an attempt in Lombard Street,' the patrol explained. 'I've heard of him.'

'I'll come down with him immediately in a cab,' said the telephone.

When Simon returned to the impregnable door of Vault 39 he listened in vain for a sound. Then he knocked with his pen-knife on the polished steel, and presently there was an answering signal from within—a series of scarcely perceptible irregular taps. It struck him that the irregularity of the taps formed a rhythm, and after a few seconds he recognised the rhythm of the Intermezzo from 'Cavalleria Rusticana,' which he had played for Hugo that very morning.

It was at this moment that the messenger-boy attached to the department came whistling into the steel corridors, and delivered to the patrol a small white packet, which, he said, Mr. Brown had handed to him with instructions to hand it to the patrol. He had seen Mr. Brown in a cab outside the building, and Mr. Brown had the appearance of being very ill.

The packet contained the second key of Vault 39.

'But this'll be no use till to-morrow,' was the patrol's comment, 'and by then—'

CHAPTER XIII

MR. GALPIN

When the patrol and Simon between them had explained the mysterious and fatal situation to Mr. Jack Galpin, Mr. Jack Galpin leaned against one of the marble tables in the waiting-room, and roared with laughter.

'Well,' observed Mr. Galpin, 'he didn't have his Safe Deposit built for nothing, anyhow!'

And he laughed again.

'But he's slowly dying in there!' said Simon.

'Yes, I know,' said Mr. Galpin. 'That's what makes it such a good joke.'

'I don't see it, sir,' Simon remarked.

'Simply because your sense of humour is a bit off. What are you?'

'I am Mr. Hugo's man.'

'My respects.'

Mr. Galpin had arrived with Inspector Winter, and Inspector Winter had introduced him as knowing more about safes than any other man in England, or perhaps in Europe. After the introduction, Inspector Winter, being pressed for time, had departed. Mr. Galpin was aged about forty, and looked like an extremely successful commercial traveller. No one would have suspected that he had recently done eighteen months anywhere but in a first-class hotel; even his thin hands were white, and if his hair was a little short—well, the hair of very many respectable persons is often a little short. It appeared that he was under obligations to Inspector Winter, and anxious to oblige. The relations between distinguished law-breakers and distinguished detectives are frequently such as can only exist between artists who esteem each other. For the rest, Mr. Galpin had brought a brown bag.

'You see, the time-lock is placed so that—' began the patrol.

'Shut up!' said Mr. Galpin curtly. 'I know all that. I've got scale-plans of every Safe Deposit in London, and I decided long since that this one was too good to try. Of course, with the aid of the entire staff things might be a bit easier, but not much—not much!' he repeated scornfully. 'If I can manage a job at all, I can usually manage it alone, and in spite of the entire staff.'

'I suppose you couldn't burn the door of the vault with oxy-hydrogen?' Simon suggested.

'Yes, I could,' said Mr. Galpin; 'and with the brand of steel used here I should get through about this time to-morrow. I could blow the bally vault up with gun-cotton in something under two seconds, but no doubt your Mr. Hugo would go up with it, and then the Yard would be angry. No!'

He hummed an air, and strolled out into the main corridor to stare at the curious dial of the time-lock.

'Why not blow up the clock of the time-lock?' ventured the patrol.

'Look here!' said Mr. Galpin, '*you* ought to know better than that, even if this other gent doesn't. Any violence to the clock automatically jams all the connecting levers. Stop the clock, and it's all up. Nothing but unbuilding the whole place would free the locks after that. And it would be a mighty smart firm that could unbuild this place inside a fortnight. No!' he said again. 'No gammon with the clock—unless we could make it go quicker.'

'Then there's nothing,' Simon stammered.

Mr. Galpin gazed at the young man.

'Assuming I do the job, what's the job worth?' he asked.

'It's worth anything.'

'Is it worth a hundred pounds?'

'Yes.'

'Cash?'

'Yes, I promise it. I will hand you my savings-bank book if you like.'

'I only ask because I have a sort of a notion about that clock. It's a pendulum clock, and you know how fast a clock ticks when you take the pendulum away, and the escapement can run free. It does an hour in about three minutes. Now, if I could get the pendulum out without alarming the clock ... it would be nine to-morrow morning in no time. See?'

'I see that,' said the patrol. 'I see that. But what I don't see—'

'Never mind what you don't see,' Mr. Jack Galpin murmured. 'Bring me my bag out of there. I may tell you,' he went on to Simon, 'that I thought of this scheme months ago, just as a pleasant sort of a fancy, but quite practical. It's a queer world, isn't it?'

'Here's your bag,' said the patrol.

'Now you two can just go into the waiting-room, and wait till I call you. Understand? And tell all these wild beasts round here to hold their tongues and sit tight. I haven't got to be disturbed in a job like this.... And it's a hundred pounds if I do it, mister, no more and no less, eh?'

Within exactly twenty-five minutes Mr. Galpin entered the waiting-room.

'See that?' he said, holding up a pendulum. 'That's *it*. You can come and look now. But I don't invite the public to see my own private melting process. Not me!'

He had burnt two holes through the half-inch plate of Bessemer steel in which the clock was enclosed, and by means of two pairs of tweezers (which must certainly have been imitated from the armoury of a dentist) he had detached the pendulum without stopping the clock. The hands of the clock could be plainly seen to move, and its ticking was furiously rapid.

Mr. Galpin made a calculation on his dazzling cuff.

'In three-quarters of an hour the clock will have run out,' he informed his audience, 'and you will be able to open any locks that you've got keys for. I shall call to-morrow morning, young man, for the swag. And don't you forget that there's only one Jack Galpin in the world. My address is 205, the Waterloo Road.'

He left, with his bag.

Simon rushed to Vault 39 to encourage the captive by continual knocking.

Then the messenger-boy, who had been despatched to obtain food for the prisoners behind the various grilles, came back with the desired food, and with a copy of the *Evening Herald*. The back page of the *Herald* bore Hugo's immense advertisement. The front page was also chiefly devoted to Hugo. It displayed headings such as: 'Shocking Scenes at a Sloane Street Sale,' 'Women Injured,' 'Customers Complain of Wholesale Swindling,' 'Scandalous Mismanagement,' 'The Hugo Safe Deposit Suddenly Closed,' 'Reported Disappearance of Mr. Hugo,' 'Is He a Lunatic?'

And when the three-quarters of an hour had expired Simon and the patrol unlocked the massive portal of Vault 39, and swung it open, fearful of what they might see within. And Hugo, pale and feeble, but alive, staggered heavily forward, and put a hand on Simon's shoulder.

'Let us get away from this,' he whispered, as if in profound mental agony.

Ignoring everything, he passed out of the impregnable Safe Deposit, with its flashing steel walls, on Simon's obedient arm.

CHAPTER XIV

TEA

Arrived on the ground-floor, Simon managed to avoid the busy parts of the establishment, but he happened to choose a way to Hugo's private lift which led past the service-door of the Hugo Grand Central Restaurant. And Hugo, although apparently in a sort of torpor, noticed it.

'Tea!' he ejaculated. 'If I could have some at once!'

And he directed Simon into the restaurant, and so came plump upon one of the worst scenes in the entire place. The first day of the great annual sale was closing in almost a riot, and there in the restaurant the primeval and savage instincts of the vast, angry crowd were naturally to be seen in their crudest form. The famous walnut buffet, eighty feet in length, was besieged by an army of customers, chiefly women, who were competing for food in a manner which ignored even the rudiments of politeness. It would be difficult to deny that several scores of well-dressed ladies, robbed of their self-possession and their lunch by delays and vexations and impositions in the departments, were actually fighting for food. The girls behind the buffet remained nobly at their posts, but the situation had outgrown their experience. Every now and then a crash of crockery or crystal was heard over the din of shrill voices, and occasionally a loud protest. Away from the buffet, on the fine floor of the restaurant, a few waitresses hurried distracted and aimless between the tables at which sat irate and scandalized persons who firmly believed themselves to be dying of hunger. A number of people were most obviously stealing food, not merely from the sideboards, but from their fellows. At a table near to the corner in which Hugo, shocked by the spectacle, had fallen limp into a chair, was seated an old, fierce man, who looked like a retired Indian judge, and who had somehow secured a cup of tea all to himself. A pretty young woman approached him, and deliberately snatched the cup from under his very nose—and without spilling a drop. The Indian judge sprang up, roared 'Hussy!' and knocked the table over with a prodigious racket, then proceeded to pick the table up again.

'Is it like this everywhere?' asked Hugo of Shawn.

And Shawn nodded.

'I might have foreseen,' Hugo murmured.

'I'll try to get you some tea, sir,' Shawn said, with an attempt to be cheerful.

'Don't leave me,' begged Hugo, like a sick child. 'Don't leave me.'

'Only for a moment, sir,' said Shawn, departing.

Hugo felt that he was about to swoon, that he had suffered just as much as a man could suffer, and that Fate was dropping the last straw on the camel's back. His head fell forward. He was beaten for that day by too many mysteries and too many tortures. And then he observed that the pretty young woman who had stolen the cup of tea from the Indian judge was hastening towards him with the cup of tea in one hand and several pieces of bread-and-butter in the other.

'Drink this, Mr. Hugo,' she whispered, standing over him. He hesitated. *'Drink it, I say, or must I throw it over you?'*

He sipped, and sipped again, obediently.

'Good, isn't it?' she questioned.

He looked up at her. He was stronger already.

'It's very good,' he said, with conviction. 'Now a bit of bread-and-butter. Thanks.' Yes, the excellence and power of the Hugo tea was not to be denied, and he was deeply glad in that moment that he owned his private plantations in Ceylon. 'Who are you, may I ask?' he demanded of his rescuer.

'If you please, sir, I'm Albert's wife.'

'Albert?'

'Albert Shawn, your detective, sir.'

'Of course you are!'

'You gave us a bedroom suite for a wedding present, sir.'

'Of course I did! By the way, where's Albert?'

'He's had an accident to his foot, and couldn't come to-day. You're less pale than you were, sir. Take this other piece.'

Then Simon returned, empty-handed, and Lily's eye indicated to him her real opinion of the value of a male in a crisis. She asked no questions concerning the events which had ended in Hugo's collapse. She merely dealt with the collapse, and in the intervals of dealing with it she explained to Simon how she had waited and waited in the dome, and then descended and tried in vain to enter the Safe Deposit, and been insulted by the messenger-boy, and had finally drifted to the restaurant, where she had caught sight of Hugo and himself, and guessed immediately that something in the highest degree unusual had occurred.

'Come,' said Hugo at last, in curt command, 'I am better.'

He had recovered. He was Hugo again. And Simon was once more nothing but his body servant, and Lily nothing but an ex-waitress who had married rather well. He thanked Lily, and told her to go and look after her husband as well as she had looked after him.

In the dome Simon ventured to show him the *Evening Herald*. And, having read it, Hugo nodded his head and pressed his lips together. He had ordered champagne and sandwiches, and was consuming them, at the same time opening a series of yellow envelopes which lay on a table. These latter were reports from his detective corps, which had accumulated during the day.

'Get a sheet of plain paper,' he said to Simon, 'and write this letter. Are you ready? Yes, it will do in pencil; I even prefer it in pencil.

'"DEAR SIR,

'"I have reason to think that you may be interested in some extraordinary information which I have in my possession concerning Camilla Tudor, who is supposed to have been buried at Brompton Cemetery in July last year. If I am right, perhaps you will accompany the bearer to my rooms. At present I will not disclose my name.

'"Yours, etc."

'Put any initials you like. Address it to Louis Ravengar, Esquire. Now listen to me. Go down to the auto garage, and choose a good man to take the note instantly; a second man must go with him. If they bring back Ravengar, he is to be taken to No. 6, Blair Street, shown upstairs, and brought along the bridge-passage into the building. It will be quite dark, and he will never guess. If necessary, he must be brought to me by force, once he is inside. Have two or three porters in attendance to see to that. But if it's managed properly, he'll come without a suspicion, and he'll be finely surprised when he finds that the long passage ends in just this room. Come back to me as soon as you've attended to that.'

'Yes, sir,' said Simon, quite mystified, but none the less enchanted to see Hugo so actively the old Hugo.

In ten minutes he had returned, and was beginning to relate new facts which he had learnt while downstairs.

'Stop!' said Hugo. 'Don't worry me with needless details. I know enough. And don't ask me any questions. We can't hope to remedy the state of affairs to-day. Nevertheless, we can do something for to-morrow. I must have Mr. Bentley, the drapery manager, brought here before six o'clock. He must be found.'

'He is found, sir. He has shot himself in his house in Pimlico Road.'

Hugo started.

'Ah!' was all he said at first. He added dryly: 'Good! And Brown?'

'I have no news of him, sir. He's vanished.'

'Telephone down to the press department that Mr. Aked must come up to see me at seven o'clock precisely, and, in the meantime, he must secure an extra half-page in all to-morrow's papers.'

'Yes, sir.'

'And after closing-time the entire staff must assemble, the men in the carpet-rooms, and the women in the central restaurant—or what's left of it. I shall speak to them. Have notices put in the common-rooms.'

'Yes, sir.'

'And send me all the buyers from the drapery department. They must go round and buy every silvered fox-stole in London to-night, at no matter what price.'

'Certainly, sir.'

'And telephone to Y.Z. that I shall be down there as soon as I can about these things.'

He touched the pile of yellow envelopes. Y.Z. was the name always given to the detectives' private room.

'Precisely, sir.'

'That's all.'

Simon Shawn gathered that his master had a very definite clue to the origin of the unique and fatal events of that day, and that all dark places were about to be made light with a blinding light.

CHAPTER XV

RAVENGAR IN CAPTIVITY

'Ravengar, what a fool you are!'

The dome was in darkness. Hugo, who stood concealed near the switch, turned on all the lights as soon as he had uttered this singular greeting, and stepped forward. He had decided to kill Ravengar. The desire to murder was in his heart, and in order to give all his instincts full play he had chosen a theatrical method of welcoming his victim into the fastness from which he was never to escape.

'D—n!' exclaimed Ravengar, evidently astounded to the uttermost to find himself in Hugo's dome, and in the presence of Hugo.

He sprang back to the door of the dressing-room by which he had so unsuspectingly entered.

'What a fool you are to fall into a trap so simple! No; don't try to get away. You can't. That door is locked now. And, moreover, I have a revolver here, and also a pair of handcuffs, which I shall use if I have any trouble with you.'

Ravengar gazed at his captor, irresolute. His clean-shaven upper lip seemed longer than ever, and his short gray beard and gray locks gave him an appearance of sanctimony which not even his sinister eyes could destroy. Then he sat down on a chair.

'I should like to know—' he began, trying to speak steadily.

'You would like to know,' Hugo took him up, 'why I am here alive, instead of being in that vault, suffocated. It was a pretty dodge of yours to get me down there. You counted on my curiosity about the Tudor mystery. You felt sure I should yield to the temptation. And I did yield. You were right. I was prepared to commit a breach of faith in order to satisfy that curiosity. No sooner was the door closed on me by that scoundrel Brown, and I found the vault not Polycarp's vault at all, than I knew to a certainty that you were at the bottom of the affair. So easy to make out afterwards that it was an accident! So easy to spirit Brown away! So easy to explain everything! Why, Ravengar, you intended to murder me! I saw the whole scheme in a flash. You have corrupted many of my servants to-day. But you didn't corrupt all of them. And because you didn't, because you couldn't, I am alive. You would like to know how I got out. But you will never know, Ravengar. You will die without knowing.'

Ravengar put his hands in his pockets.

'I can only assume that you are going mad, Owen,' said he. 'I have long guessed that you were. Nothing else will explain this extraordinary action of yours towards me.'

'You act well,' replied Hugo, sitting down and eyeing Ravengar critically. 'You act well. But you gave the whole show away by the tone in which you swore two minutes ago. If there is anyone mad in this room, it is yourself. Your schemes show that queer mixture of amazing ingenuity and amazing folly which is characteristic of madmen. Let us hope you are mad, at any rate.'

'My schemes!' sneered Ravengar. 'You might at least tell the madman what his schemes are.'

Hugo laughed.

'You must have been maturing the day's business quite a long time, my boyhood's companion, my floater of public companies, my pearl of financiers. Yes, decidedly parts of it were wonderfully ingenious. To sow the place with pickpockets, to get at my cashiers, my commissionaires, and my servers. To substitute your own false shopwalkers for the genuine article. To arrange for the arrest of important customers on preposterous charges of theft. To lock up a hundred women in a gallery till they nearly died. To have my best and most advertised bargains removed in the night. To deprive the restaurants of food, and to employ women to turn them upside down. To produce, as you contrived to do, a general air of pandemonium, and to ruin the discipline of over three thousand of the best-trained employés in England. All this, and much else which I do not mention, was devilish clever in its conception, and the execution of it commands my unqualified admiration. Especially having regard to the fact that you contrived not to arouse my suspicions. I may tell you that certain strange incidents which occurred in my establishment during the autumn did indeed lead me vaguely to suspect that you were at work against me, but you were sufficiently smart to put me off the track again. Let me add that until this afternoon I did not perceive that your purchase of a controlling share in the *Evening Herald* was only a portion of a mightier plan.'

'Really, Owen—'

'Don't waste your breath in denials. You will have none at all presently, like Bentley.'

'Bentley?' repeated Ravengar, with a slight movement.

'Yes; but we will come to Bentley in a few minutes. I have enlarged to you on your own cleverness. I must enlarge to you on your folly. What folly! What was the end of all this to be, Ravengar? I have tried to put myself in your place, and to follow your thoughts. You hate me. You think I robbed you of a fortune, and that I helped to rob you of a woman. You wished to buy my business, and add it to the roll of your companies. And I deprived you of that triumph. Your hatred of me grew and grew. Leading a solitary and narrow life, you allowed it to develop into a species of monomania. I had come out on top once too often for your peace of mind. In your opinion the world was too small to hold both of us. Accordingly, you evolved your terrific campaign. My business was to be seriously damaged. And I was to be murdered. And then you were to get the concern cheap from my executors, and to float me dead since you could not float me living. What folly, Ravengar! What stupendous folly! Even if the fanciful and grotesque scheme had succeeded as far as my death, it could not have succeeded beyond that point.'

'I don't know what you are chattering about, Owen, but you look as if you expected me to ask, "Why?" Anything to oblige you. Why?'

'You would have known the reason had you lived long enough to read the provisions of my will,' said Hugo.

'I see,' said Ravengar.

'You do,' said Hugo. 'You see, you hear, you breathe, but Bentley doesn't. Bentley has killed himself.' (Ravengar started.) 'So that if you have not my blood on your conscience, you have his. You tempted him; he fell ... and he has repented. Admit that you tempted him!'

Ravengar smiled superiorly. And then Hugo sprang forward in a sudden overmastering passion.

'Hate breeds hate,' he cried, 'and I have learnt from you how to hate. Admit that you have tried to ruin and to murder me, or, by G—! I will kill you sooner than I intended.'

He had no weapon in his hands; the revolver was in a drawer; but nevertheless Ravengar shrank from those menacing hands.

'Look here, Hugo—'

'Will you admit it? Or shall I have to—'

Their wills met in a supreme conflict.

'Oh, very well, then,' muttered Ravengar.

The conflict was over.

Hugo returned to his chair.

'Miserable cur!' he exclaimed. 'You were afraid of me. I knew I could frighten you. I would have liked to be able to admire something more than your ingenuity. Ravengar, I do believe I could have forgiven your attempt to murder me if it had not included an attempt to dishonour me at the same time. There is something simple and grand about a straightforward murder—I shall prove to you soon that I do not always regard murder as a crime—but to murder a man amid circumstances of shame, to finish him off while making him look a fool—that is the act of a—of a Ravengar.'

Ravengar yawned and glanced at his watch.

'It's nearly my dinner-time,' said he.

Again Hugo sprang forward, and, snatching at the watch, tore it and the chain from Ravengar's waistcoat, dashed them to the floor, and stamped on them. He was amazed, and he was also delighted, at his own fury. The lust of destruction had got hold of him.

'Ass!' he murmured, suddenly lowering his voice. 'Can't you guess what I mean to do?'

'I cannot,' Ravengar stammered.

'I mean to put you to the same test to which you put me. You arranged that I should spend twenty-two hours in a vault without ventilation. At the end of five hours I was by no means dead. I might have survived the twenty-two. But, frankly, I don't fancy I should. And I don't fancy you will. In fact, I'm convinced that you won't.'

'Indeed!' said Ravengar uncertainly.

'You think this scene is not real,' Hugo continued. 'You think it can't be real. You refuse to credit the fact that this time to-morrow you will be dead. You refuse to admit to yourself that I am in earnest—deadly, fatal earnest.'

'Upon my soul!' Ravengar burst out, standing, 'I believe you are.'

'Good,' said Hugo. 'You are waking up, positively. You are getting accustomed to the unpleasant prospect of not dying in your bed surrounded by inconsolable dependants.'

'Hugo,' Ravengar began persuasively, 'you must be aware that all these suspicions of yours are a figment of your excited brain. You must be aware that I never meant to murder you.'

'My dear fellow,' Hugo replied with calm bitterness, '*I* don't intend to murder *you*. I intend merely to put you in that vault. Your death will be an accidental consequence, as mine would have been. And why should you not die? Can you give me a single good reason why you should continue to live? What good are you doing on the earth? Are you making anyone happy? Are you making yourself happy? That spark of vitality which constitutes your soul has chanced on an unfortunate incarnation. Suppose that I release it, and give it a fresh opportunity, shall I not be acting worthily? For you must agree that murder in the strict sense is an impossible thing. The immortal cannot die. Vital energy cannot be destroyed. All that the murderer does is to end one incarnation and begin another.'

'So that is your theory!'

'Was it not yours, when you got me deposited in the vault?' Hugo demanded with ferocious irony. 'I am bound to believe that it was. The common outcry against murder (as it is called) can have no weight with enlightened persons like you and me, Ravengar.'

'Perhaps not,' said Ravengar, summoning his powers of self-control. 'But the common outcry against murder is apt to be very inconvenient for the person who chooses, as you put it, to end one incarnation and begin another. Has it not struck you, Owen, that inquiries would be made for me, that my death would be certain to be discovered, and that ultimately you would suffer the penalty?'

'My arrangements for the future are far more complete than yours could have been in regard to me,' Hugo answered smoothly. 'You betrayed some clumsiness. I shall profit by your mistakes. No one will see you go into the Safe Deposit except myself and a man whom I can trust. No one at all except myself will see you go into the vault. I can manage the operation alone. A little chloroform will quieten you for a time. The vault once closed will not be opened during my lifetime, unless at four o'clock to-morrow night I hear you knocking on the door. Of course, inquiries will be made, but they will be futile. People often simply disappear. You will simply disappear.'

The clock struck six.

'And your conscience?' Ravengar muttered.

'It's soon well under control. Besides, I shall be doing the human race, and especially the investing part of the human race, a very good turn.'

Then Ravengar approached Hugo, and, Hugo rising to meet him, their faces almost touched in the middle of the great room.

'You called me a cur,' he said. 'Yet perhaps I am not such a cur after all. You have beaten me. You mean to finish me; I can see it in your face. Well, you will regret it more than I shall. Do you know I have often wished to die? You are right in saying that there is no reason why I should live. I am only a curse to the world. But you are wrong to scorn me when you kill me. You ought to pity me. Did I choose my temperament, my individuality? As I am, so I was born, and from his character no man can escape.'

And he sat down, and Hugo sat down.

'When is it to be?' Ravengar questioned.

'In a few minutes,' said Hugo impassively, feeding his mortal resentment on the memory of those hours when he himself had waited for death in the vault.

'Then I shall have time to ask you how you came to know that Camilla Payne, or rather Camilla Tudor, is alive.'

'She is not alive,' Hugo explained. 'The suggestion contained in my decoy letter was a pure invention in order to entice you. As you tempted me into the vault, so I tempted you here on your way to the vault.'

'But she is alive all the same!' Ravengar persisted. 'It is the fact that she is not dead that makes me less unwilling to die, for a word from her might send me to a death more shameful than the one you have so kindly arranged for me.'

Hugo in that instant admired Ravengar, and he replied quite gently:

'You are mistaken. Where can you have got the idea that she is not dead? She is dead. I myself—I myself screwed her up in her coffin.'

The words sounded horrible.

'Then you were in the plot!' Ravengar cried.

'What plot?'

'The plot to persuade me falsely that she is dead. Bah! I know more than you think. I know, for example, that her body is not in the coffin in Brompton Cemetery. And I am almost sure that I know where she is hiding. I should have known beyond doubt before to-morrow morning. However, what does it matter now?'

'Not in the coffin?' Hugo whispered, as if to himself. His whole frame trembled, shook, and his heart, leaping, defied his intellect.

CHAPTER XVI

BURGLARS

When at eleven o'clock that same winter night Hugo stood hesitating, with certain tools and a hooded electric lamp in his hand, on the balcony in front of the drawing-room window of Francis Tudor's sealed flat, he thought what a strange, illogical, and capricious thing is the human heart.

He knew that Camilla was dead. He had had the very best and most convincing evidence of the fact. He knew that Ravengar's suspicions were without foundation, utterly wrong-headed; and yet those statements of his enemy had unsettled him. They had not unsettled the belief of his intelligence, but they had unsettled his soul's peace. And that curiosity to learn the whole truth about the history of the relations between Francis Tudor and Camilla, that curiosity which had slumbered for months, and which had been so suddenly awakened by Ravengar's lure of the morning, was now urged into a violent activity.

Nor was this all. Camilla was surely dead. But supposing that by some incredible chance she was not dead (lo! the human heart), could he kill Ravengar? This question had presented itself to him as he sat in the dome listening to Ravengar's asseverations that Camilla lived. And the mere ridiculous, groundless suspicion that she lived, the mere fanciful dream that she lived, had quite changed and softened Hugo's mood. He had struggled hard to keep his resolution to kill Ravengar, but it had melted away; he had fanned the fire of his mortal hatred, but it had cooled, and at length he had admitted to himself, angrily, reluctantly, that Ravengar had escaped the ordeal of the vault. And this being decided, what could he do with Ravengar? Retain him under lock and key? Why? To what end? Such illegal captivities were not practicable for long in London. Besides, they were absurd, melodramatic, and futile. As the moments passed and the fumes of a murderous intoxication gradually cleared away, Hugo had regained his natural, sagacious perspective, and he had perceived that there was only one thing to do with Ravengar.

He let Ravengar go. He showed him politely out.

It was an anti-climax, but the incalculable and peremptory processes of the heart often result in an anti-climax.

The night was cold and damp, as the morning had been, and Hugo shivered, but not with cold. He shivered in the mere exciting eagerness of anticipation. He had chosen the drawing-room window because the panes were very large. He found it perfectly simple, by means of the treacled cardboard which he carried, to force in the pane noiselessly. He pushed aside the blind, and crept within the room. So simple was it to violate the will of a dead man, and the solemnly affixed seals of his executor! He had arranged that the pane should be replaced before dawn, and the new putty darkened to match the rest. Thus, no trace would remain of the burglarious entry. No seal on door or window would have been broken.

He stood upright in the drawing-room, restored the blind and the heavy curtains to their positions, and then ventured to press the button of his lamp. He saw once more the vast outlines of the room which he had last seen under such circumstances of woe. The great pieces of furniture were enveloped in holland covers, and resembled formless ghosts in the pale illumination of the lamp. He shivered again. He was afraid now, with the fear of the unknown, the forbidden, and the withheld. Why was he there? What could he hope to discover?

In answer to these questions, he replied:

'Why did Francis Tudor order that the flat should be closed? He must have had some reason. I will find it out. It is essential to my peace of mind to know. I meant to commit murder to-day; I have only committed burglary. I ought to congratulate myself and sing for joy, instead of feeling afraid.'

So he reassured his spirit as he stepped carefully into the midst of the holland-covered and moveless ghosts. On the mantelpiece to the left there still stood the electric table-light, and by its side still lay the screwdriver.... He determined to pass straight through the drawing-room. At the further edge of the carpet, on the parquet flooring between the carpet and the portière leading to the inner hall, he noticed under the ray of his lamp footprints in the dust—footprints of a man, and smaller footprints, either of a woman or a child. He remained motionless, staring at them. Then it occurred to him that during the days between the death of its tenant and the sealing-up the flat would probably not have been cleaned, and that these footprints must have been made months ago by the last persons to leave the flat. Little dust would fall after the closing of the flat. He was glad that he had thought of that explanation. It was a convincing explanation.

Nevertheless he dared not proceed. For on the other mantelpiece to the right there was a clock, and while staring in the ghostly silence at the footprints, he had fancied that his ear caught the ticking of the clock. Imagination, doubtless! But he dared not proceed until he had satisfied himself that his ears had deluded him; and, equally, he dared not approach the clock to satisfy himself. He could only gaze at the reflection of the clock in the opposite mirror. In the opposite mirror the hands indicated half a minute past nine; hence the clock was really at half a minute to three, and if it was actually going, it might be expected to strike immediately. He waited. He heard a preliminary grinding noise familiar to students of symptoms in clocks, and in the fraction of a second he was bathed from head to foot in a cold perspiration.

The clock struck three.

The next instant he walked boldly up to the clock and bent his ear to it. No, he could hear nothing. It had stopped. He glared steadily at the hands for two minutes by his own watch; they did not move.

In the back of his head, in the small of his back, in his legs, little tracts of his epidermis tickled momentarily. He wiped his face, and walked boldly away from the clock to the portière, which he lifted with one arm. Then he threw the light of his lamp direct on the dial, and glared at it again, fearful lest it should have taken advantage of his departure to resume its measuring of eternity.

Could a clock go for four months? A clock could be made that would go for four months. But this was not a freak-clock. It was a large Louis Seize pendule, and he knew it to be genuine of his own knowledge; he had bought it.

He dropped the portière between himself and the clock, and stood in the inner hall. He had had as much of the drawing-room as was good for his nerves.

The inner hall was oblong in shape, and measured about twelve feet at its greatest width. In front of him, as he stood with his back to the drawing-room, was a closed door, which he knew led into the principal bedroom of the flat. To his right another heavy portière divided the inner from the outer hall. This portière hung in straight perpendicular folds. He wondered why the portières had not been taken down and folded away.

He decided to penetrate first into the bedroom, partly because he deemed the bedroom might contain the solution of the enigma, and partly because his eye had fancied it saw a slight tremor in the portière leading to the outer hall. So he stepped stoutly across the space which separated him from the bedroom door. But he had not reached the door before there was a loud, sharp explosion, and a panel of the door splintered and showed a hole, and he thought he heard a faint cry.

A revolver shot!

He did not believe in anything so far-fetched as man-traps and spring-guns. Hence there must be some person or persons in the flat. Some unseen intelligence was following him. Some mysterious will had ordained that he should not enter that bedroom. The shot was a warning. He guessed from the flight of the splinters and the appearance of the hole that the mysterious will must be on the other side of the portière, but the portière gave no sign.

What was he to do? He had brought with him no weapon. He had not anticipated that revolvers would be needed in the exploration of an empty and forbidden flat. The very definite terrors of the inner hall seemed to him to surpass the vaguer terrors of the drawing-room, and he decided to return thither in order to consider quietly what his tactics should be; if necessary, he could return to the dome for arms and assistance. But no sooner did he move a foot towards the drawing-room than another shot sounded. The drawing-room portière trembled, and something crashed within the apartment. The mysterious will had ardently decided that he should go neither back nor forward.

'Who's there? Who's that shooting?' he muttered thickly, and extinguished his lamp.

He had meant to cry out loud, but, to his intense surprise, his throat was dried up.

There was no answer, no stir, no noise. The silence that exists between the stars seemed to close in upon him. Then he really knew what fear was. He admitted to himself that he was unmistakably and horribly afraid. He admitted that life was inconceivably precious, and the instinct to preserve it the greatest of all instincts. And gradually he came to see that the safest course was the most desperate course, and gradually his courage triumphed over his fear.

He dropped gently to his hands and knees, and began, with a thousand precautions, to crawl like a serpent towards the outer hall. The darkened lamp he held between his teeth. If the mysterious will fired again, the mysterious will would almost to a certainty fire harmlessly over his head. At last his hands touched the portière. He hesitated, listened, and put one hand under the portière. Then, relighting the lamp, he sprang up with a yell on the other side of the portière, and clutched for the unseen intelligence.

But there was nothing. He stood alone in the outer hall. To his right lay the side-passage between the drawing-room and the *cabinet de toilette,* which Camilla had used on the night of her engagement. In front of him was a door, slightly ajar, which led to the servants' quarters. He gazed around, breathing heavily.

CHAPTER XVII

POLYCARP AND HAWKE'S MAN

Then it was that he heard a noise, something between scratching and fumbling, on the further side of the front-door, in the main corridor of the flats. He could see through the ground glass over the door that the corridor was lighted as usual.

He thought: 'Someone is breaking the seal on that door!' And his next idea was: 'Since the seal is being broken in the full light of the public corridor, it is being broken by someone who has the right to break it. Only one man has the right, and that man is Francis Tudor's executor, Senior Polycarp.'

The noise of scratching and fumbling ceased, and a key was placed in the lock.

Hugo hastily extinguished his lamp, and hid behind the portière. Immediately the lamp was extinguished he observed, what he had not observed before, that a faint light came through the aperture of the door leading to the servants' quarters.

The front-door opened, and he heard footsteps in the hall. Then ensued a pause. Then the footsteps advanced, and the newcomer evidently went into the room where the faint light was.

'Come out of that!'

Yes; it was Polycarp's quiet, mincing, imperious voice.

'Come out of it yourself!'

The answering tones were gruff, heavy, full, the speech of a strong coarse-fibred man.

Hugo peeped cautiously through the portière. Polycarp was backing slowly out of the room into the hall, followed by a tall, dark, scowling man, who bore an ordinary kitchen candle. Polycarp halted in the middle of the floor. The man also halted; he seemed to be towering over Polycarp in an attitude of menace.

'Let me pass,' said the man. 'I've had enough of this.'

Polycarp smiled scornfully.

'You're caught,' said he. 'You're one of Hawke's men, aren't you?'

'Go to h—!' was the man's ferocious reply.

'Answer my question, sir.'

'What if I am?' the man grumbled.

'In five minutes you'll be in the hands of the police. I got wind yesterday of what your rascally agency was up to. You needn't deny anything. You're working on behalf of Mr. Ravengar. You know me! Mr. Ravengar happens to be a client of mine, but after to-night he will be so no longer. What he wants done in this flat I cannot guess, but it's an absolute certainty that you're in for three years' penal, my friend.'

'Let me pass,' the man repeated, lifting his jaw, 'or I'll blow your brains out!'

He produced his revolver.

'Oh no, you won't,' said Polycarp coldly. 'You daren't. You aren't on the stage, and you aren't in Texas. And you aren't a bold Bret Harte villain. You're simply the creature of a private inquiry agency, as it's called, the most miserable of trades! Usually you spend your time in manufacturing divorces, but just now you're doing something more dangerous even than that, something that needed more pluck than you've got. I should advise you to come with me quietly.'

Polycarp was in evening dress, and carried a pair of white gloves. Hugo decidedly admired the old dandy as he stood there gazing up so condescendingly at the man with the candle.

'Look here!' said the man with the candle. 'Let me pass. I don't want any fuss. I want to go. There's more in this flat than I bargained for. Let me pass.'

'Give me that revolver,' Polycarp smoothly demanded.

'Curse it!' cried the man. 'I'll give it you! Hands up, you old fool! Do you think I'm here for fun?'

And he raised the revolver.

'I shall not put my hands up.'

'I'll count five,' said the man grimly, 'and if you don't—'

'Count.'

'One!... two!... three! Can't you see I mean it?'

Hugo perceived plainly the murderous, wild look on the man's face. He knew what it was to feel murderous. He knew that in a fit of homicide all considerations of prudence, all care for the future, vanish away, that the mind is utterly monopolized by the obsession of the one single desire.

Polycarp disdainfully sneered:

'Four!'

Hugo could withstand the strain no more. He bounded out from his concealment, and snatched the revolver from the man's hand.

'I forgot you,' growled the man, glancing at him, disgusted.

And so saying he dashed the candle in Polycarp's face and knocked him violently against Hugo. Both Hugo and Polycarp fell to the ground. The man made a leap for the door, and in a second had fled, banging it after him. Hugo and Polycarp rose with stiff movements. Hugo picked up his lamp, and the two confronted each other. It was a highly delicate situation.

'Your life is, at any rate, saved,' said Hugo at length.

'You think it was in danger?'

Polycarp's lip curled.

'I think so.'

'Possibly you foresaw the danger I ran,' Polycarp remarked with frigid irony, 'and came into the flat with the intention of protecting me. May I ask *how* you came in?'

'I came in through the drawing-room window,' said Hugo. 'I did not interfere with your seals, however,' he added.

'You know you are guilty of a criminal offence?'

'I know it.'

'And that I, as executor of the late Francis Tudor, have a duty which I must perform, no matter how unpleasant both for you and for me?'

'Just so.'

'What are you doing here? Do you think your conduct is worthy of a gentleman?'

Hugo put the candle down on a table, and dug his hands into his pockets.

'At this moment,' said he, 'I am not a gentleman. I am just a man. Nothing else. I will appeal to you as another man. I need hardly say that I have no connection with the opposition firm; I was entirely ignorant of the presence of Hawke's mission here when I broke into the flat. I had no notion that Ravengar was pursuing investigations similar to mine. Mr. Polycarp, Ravengar is, or was, a client of yours—'

'Was.'

'Yes, I heard what you said a few moments ago. Was a client of yours. I am sure, therefore, that no one knows better than you that Ravengar is not an honest man. On the other hand, I am equally sure that on the few occasions when you and I have met I must have impressed you as a comparatively honest man. Is it not so? I speak without false modesty. Is it not so?'

Polycarp nodded.

'Well, then,' proceeded Hugo, walking slowly about, 'you will probably need no convincing that in any difficulty between me and Ravengar I am in the right. Now, there have been, and are, matters between Ravengar and me in which others had best not interfere, even indirectly. I shall end those matters in my own way, because I am the strongest, and because my hands are clean. I can give you no details. But let me tell you that once the whole of my life's dream was in this flat, this flat which you have legally closed, and I have illegally opened. Let me tell you that my life, the only part of my life for which I cared, came to an end in this flat some months ago: and that a mystery hangs over that event which has lately made intolerable even the dead-alive existence which Fate had left to me. Let me tell you that circumstances have arisen this very day which rendered it impossible for me to keep myself out of this flat, be the penalty what it might. And, finally, let me make my appeal to you.'

'What do you want?' asked Polycarp quietly. The sincerity of Hugo's emotion had touched him. 'Don't ask me to act contrary to my duty.'

'But that is just what I shall ask!' Hugo exclaimed. 'Leave me. Leave me till to-morrow: that is my sole wish. What is your duty, after all? Tudor is dead. He is beyond the reach of harm. He requires the protection of no lawyer. Trust me, and leave me. I am an honest man. Forget your law, forget your parchments, forget the conventions of society, forget everything except that you are human, and can do a service to a fellow-creature. Exercise some imagination, and see how artificial and absurd is the world of ideas in which you live. Listen to your heart, and help me. I am worth it. Can't you see how I suffer? To-day I have been through as much as I can stand. I am at the end of my forces, and I must have sympathy. You will be guilty of deliberate neglect of duty in leaving me here, but I implore you to leave me. And I give no specific reason why you should. Will you?'

There was a silence.

'Yes,' said Polycarp.

'I thank you.'

'I don't know why I should consent,' Polycarp continued, 'but I do. I am quite in the dark. Legally, I am a disgrace to my profession. I forfeit my professional honour. But I will consent. Do what you like. Go out as you came in and leave no trace. If, however—'

'Don't trouble to say that,' Hugo interrupted him. 'I shall take no unfair advantage of your generosity. The flat and all its contents are absolutely safe in my hands. And if you should decide, in the future, that I must accept the consequences of to-night's work, I shall not shuffle. All I want is to be left alone *now*.'

Polycarp opened the door.

'Good-night,' he said. 'Perhaps you did save my life. But if you had appealed on that account to my gratitude I should have been obliged to refuse your request.'

'I know it,' said Hugo. 'I knew whom I was talking to. Good-night, and thanks.'

'I shall lock this door,' Polycarp called out, departing.

'Yes, do; and, I say, you'll lay hands on that man of Hawke's easily enough in a day or two.'

'Oh, certainly,' said Polycarp. 'I have not forgotten him. But I was compelled to deal with you first.'

Twisting his white moustache, and buttoning his overcoat across the vast acreage of his shirt-front, Polycarp disappeared from Hugo's view into the corridor.

CHAPTER XVIII

HUSBAND AND WIFE

Hugo bolted the front-door on the inside, relighted the candle which Hawke's man had used as a weapon, and placed it in the middle of the hall floor. He then penetrated into the servants' part of the flat, and emerged on to the balcony by the small side-door, which was open, and had evidently been forced by Hawke's man. And there, on the balcony, he leaned over the balustrade in the cold humid night, and tried to recover his calmness. He felt that any systematic, scientific search of the premises would be impossible to him until his mind resembled somewhat less a sea across which a hurricane has just passed.

Many questions stood ready to puzzle his brain, but he ignored them all, and fell into a vague reverie, of which Camilla was the centre. And from this reverie he was suddenly startled by the clear, unmistakable sound of a door being shut within the flat. It was not the shutting of a door by the wind, but the careful, precise shutting of a door by some person who had a habit of shutting doors as doors ought to be shut.

'Polycarp has returned!' was his first thought. But he remembered. 'No! I bolted the front-door on the inside.'

The conundrum of the clock and of the two sizes of footprints in the drawing-room recurred to him. Without allowing himself to hesitate, he strode back again into the flat, with a sort of unbreathed sigh, an unuttered complaint against circumstances for not giving him an instant's peace.

The candle was still placidly burning in the hall, but its position had certainly been shifted by at least three feet. It was much nearer the portière leading to the inner hall. Hugo listened intently. Not a sound! And he stared interrogatively at the candle as though the candle were a guilty thing.

However, he now possessed the revolver of Hawke's man, and this gave him confidence. He left the perambulating candle to itself, and proceeded to the inner hall by the light of his own electric lamp. The door of the principal bedroom, which he had originally meant to invade, lay to his right; the entrance to the drawing-room lay to his left. He thought he would take another look at the drawing-room, and then he thought:

'No; I'll tackle the bedroom.'

And he seized the handle of the bedroom door. At the first trial it would not turn, but in a moment it turned a little, and then turned back against his pressure.

'Someone's got hold of it inside!' he said to himself.

He put the lamp on a chair, and took the revolver from his pocket in readiness for any complications that might follow his forcing of the door.

Then he heard a woman's voice within the bedroom.

'I shall open it, Alb, if you kill me for it. I don't care who it is. You may be dying of loss of blood. In fact, I'm sure you are.'

And the door was pulled wide open with a single sweeping movement, and Hugo beheld the figure, slightly dishevelled and more than slightly perturbed, of Mrs. Albert Shawn.

'Oh, Alb!' cried Lily. 'It's Mr. Hugo! Oh, Mr. Hugo! whatever next will happen in this world?'

The swift loosing of the tension of Hugo's nerves was too much for his self-possession. He burst into a peal of loud laughter. It was unnaturally loud, it was hysterical; but it was genuine laughter, and it did him good.

Lily straightened herself. So far, she had not admitted Hugo into the chamber.

'It's all very well for you to laugh like that, Mr. Hugo,' she protested sharply; 'but perhaps you don't know that you've nearly killed my husband with that there revolver. The shot came through the door, and took him in the arm just as he was emptying this safe.'

Hugo saw Albert Shawn lying on the stripped bed, a handkerchief tied round his arm, and in the corner near the door a large safe opened, and its contents in a heap on the floor.

'It's all right, sir,' said Albert; 'come in. I'm nowhere near croaking. I didn't know you were on this lay as well as me, sir. I thought I was going to come down on you to-morrow with a surprise like a thousand of bricks.'

'What lay, Albert?' asked Hugo, advancing into the room.

'The secret-finding lay, sir,' said Albert.

'Your wife has the right to be anxious about you,' Hugo observed, after a pause. 'But you don't seem to be quite dying, Shawn; and I think it will be as well if you explain to me why you have adopted the profession of burglar. It is extremely singular that there should have been three burglars here to-night. You, and then me—'

'What did I tell you, Alb?' Mrs. Albert Shawn exclaimed. 'Didn't I tell you I heard a scuffle?'

'The scuffle was between me and No. 3. And be it known to you, Mrs. Shawn, that the revolver was not fired by me, but by No. 3. I took it off him, afterwards.'

'Then No. 3 must have come on behalf of Mr. Ravengar, sir,' said Albert.

'You are no doubt right,' Hugo agreed. 'But how did you know that?'

'Hawke's Detective Agency, sir. I found out before my wedding that one of their men had been hanging about here, so I chummed up to him. I spun him a yarn how I'd been with Hawke's once, and they gave me the bag, and I wasn't satisfied, and he'd got a lot of grievances against Hawke's, too, he had. We got very friendly. Pity I had to leave the thing for my wedding. But I came back after a week.'

'Yes, that he did, sir,' said Lily proudly, 'and insisted on it.'

'I soon knew they were going to burglarize this flat to get some phonograph records.'

'Phonograph records!' Hugo repeated, pondering.

'Yes, sir; and so I thought I'd be beforehand with 'em.'

'Why didn't you tell me directly you knew?'

'You gave me that Gaboriau book to read, sir, and I learnt a lot from it. It's put me up to a power of things. And, amongst others, that two people can't manage one job. One job, one man.'

'You'll excuse Albert, sir,' said Lily; 'that's only his way of talking.'

'It was simply this, sir. I found out enough to make me as sure as eggs is eggs that you'd like to have those phonograph records yourself, without having to inquire too much where they came from or how they came.'

'I see.'

'Exactly, sir. Well, to cut a long story short, sir, I happened to come across something yesterday that made me think that the annual sale was going to be interfered with by parties unknown. But I'd got all I could manage, and I left that alone; I'd no time for it. And last night parties unknown tried to break my leg for me with an open cellar-flap. I knew it was a plant, and so I pretended it had succeeded.'

'He made me think his ankle was that sprained he couldn't walk. He wouldn't trust even me, sir,' said Lily.

'Gaboriau,' Albert explained briefly. 'I knew I was watched, and I told Lily to tell the milkman I couldn't walk. It was all over Radipole Road at eight o'clock this morning. And so, while parties unknown thought I was fast on a sofa, I slipped out by the back-door as soon as I'd sent Lily here to warn you about the annual sale, in case of necessity. I must say I thought I should be twenty-four hours in front of Hawke's men, but I expect they changed their plans. I brought Lily along with me at the last moment. She's read Gaboriau, too, sir, and she's mighty handy.'

'I am aware of it,' said Hugo.

'Anyhow, we got in here first, by the side-door on the balcony. Hawke's man must have come in about an hour after us, and you just after him. That's how I reckon it.'

'You went into the drawing-room, didn't you?' Hugo asked.

'Just looked in.'

'And played with the clock?'

Here he glanced sternly at Lily.

'I shook it to start it, sir, to see if it would go,' Lily admitted.

'I reckon you turned out Hawke's man, sir?' Albert queried.

'It amounted to that,' said Hugo. 'But these phonograph records—what are they?'

'I don't know what they are,' said Albert, descending from the bed, 'but I know that Mr. Ravengar wanted them very badly. It seems Mr. Tudor was a great hand at phonographs and gramophones. Like me, sir.'

'Yes, sir; we've got a beauty. My uncle gave it us,' Lily put in. 'Oh, Alb! your arm's all burst out again.'

The bandage was, in fact, slightly discoloured.

'Oh, that's nothing, my dear,' said Albert.

He pushed up a pile of discs from in front of the safe, and displayed them to Hugo.

'Can we try them here?' Hugo demanded, in a voice suddenly and profoundly eager.

'Certainly, sir. Here's the machine. You undo this catch, and then you—'

Albert was mounted on his latest hobby, and in a few minutes, although he could only use one arm, the phonograph, which stood on the table near the safe, was ready for its work of reproduction. Albert started it.

'Follow me, follow me!'

It began to sing the famous ditty in the famous voice of Miss Edna May.

'Stop that!' cried Hugo, and Albert stopped it.

The next two discs proved to be respectively a series of stories of Mr. R.G. Knowles and 'The Lost Chord,' played on a cornet. And these also were cut short. Then came a bundle of discs tied together. Hugo himself fixed the top one, and the machine, after whirring inarticulately, said in slow, clear tones:

'In case I should die before—'

Hugo arrested the action.

'Go,' he said, almost threateningly, to Albert and his wife. 'Mrs. Shawn, look after your husband's wound. It needs it. See the blood!'

'But—'

'Go,' said Hugo.

And they went.

And when they were gone he released the mechanism, and in the still solitude of the bedroom listened to the strange story of Francis Tudor, related in Francis Tudor's own voice. It occurred to him that the man must have been talking into a phonograph shortly before he died. He remembered the monotonous voice on that fatal night in August.

CHAPTER XIX

WHAT THE PHONOGRAPH SAID

In case I should die before I can complete my arrangements for the future (said the phonograph, reproducing the voice of Francis Tudor), I am making a brief statement of the whole case into this phonograph. I am exhausted with to-day's work, and I shall find it easier and much quicker to speak than to write; and I'm informed that I ought never to exert myself more than is necessary. Supposing I were to die within the next few days—and I have yet to go through the business of the funeral ceremonies!—circumstances might arise which might nullify part of my plan, unless a clear account of the affair should ultimately come into the hands of some person whom I could trust not to make a fool of himself—such as Polycarp, my solicitor, for instance.

Hence I relate the facts for a private record.

When I first met Camilla Payne she was shorthand clerk or private secretary, or whatever you call it, to Louis Ravengar. I saw her in his office. Curiously, she didn't make a tremendous impression on me at the moment. By the way, Polycarp, if it is indeed you who listen to this, you must excuse my way of relating the facts. I can only tell the tale in my own way. Besides meddling with finance, I've dabbled in pretty nearly all the arts, including the art of fiction, and I can't leave out the really interesting pieces of my narrative merely because you're a lawyer and hate needless details, sentimental or otherwise. But *do* you hate sentimental details? I don't know. Anyhow, this isn't a counsel's brief. What was I saying? Oh! She didn't make a tremendous impression on me at the moment, but I thought of her afterwards. I thought of her a good deal in a quiet way after I had left her—so much so that I made a special journey to Ravengar's a few days afterwards, when there was no real need for me to go, in order to have a look at her face again. I should explain that I was dabbling in finance just then, fairly successfully, and had transactions with Ravengar. He didn't know that I was the son of the man who had taken his stepmother away from his father, and I never told him I had changed my name, because the scandals attached to it by Ravengar and his father had made things very unpleasant for any bearer of that name. Still, Ravengar happened to be the man I wanted to deal with, and so I didn't let any stupid resentment on my part stop me from dealing with him. He was a scoundrel, but he played the game, I may incidentally mention. I venture to give this frank opinion about one of your most important clients, because he'll be dead before you read this, Polycarp. At least, I expect so.

Well, the day I called specially with a view to seeing her she was not there. She had left Ravengar's employment, and disappeared. Ravengar seemed to be rather perturbed about it. But perhaps he was perturbed about the suicide which had recently taken place in his office. I felt it—I mean I felt her disappearance. However, the memory of her face gave me something very charming to fall back on in moments of depression, and it was at this time something occurred sufficient to make me profoundly depressed for the remainder of my life. I was over in Paris, and seeing a good deal of Darcy, my friend the English doctor there. We were having a long yarn one night in his rooms over the Café Américain, and he said to me suddenly: 'Look here, old chap, I'm going to do something very unprofessional, because I fancy you'll thank me for it.' He said it just like that, bursting out all of a sudden. So I said, 'Well?' He said: 'It's very serious, and in nine hundred and ninety-nine cases out of a thousand I should be a blundering idiot to tell you.' I said to him: 'You've begun. Finish. And let's see whether I'll thank you.' He then told me that I'd got malignant disease of the heart, might die at any moment, and in any case couldn't live more than a few years. He said: 'I thought you'd like to know, so that you could arrange your life accordingly.' I thanked him. I was really most awfully obliged to him. It wanted some pluck to tell me. He said: 'I wouldn't admit to anyone else that I'd told you.' I never admired Darcy more than I did that night. His tone was so finely casual.

In something like a month I had got used to the idea of being condemned to death. At any rate, it ceased to interfere with my sleep. I purchased a vault for myself in Brompton Cemetery. Then I took this flat that I'm talking in now, and began deliberately to think over how I should finish my life. I'd got money—much more than old Ravengar imagined —and I'm a bit of a philosopher, you know; I have my theories as to what constitutes real living. However, I won't bother you with those. I expect they're pretty crude, after all. Besides, my preparations were all knocked on the head. I saw Camilla Payne again in Hugo's. She had stopped typewriting, and was a milliner there. I tried my level best to strike up an intimacy with her, but I failed. She wouldn't have it. The fact is, I was too rich and showy. And I had a reputation behind me which, possibly—well, you're aware of all that, Polycarp. In about a fortnight I worshipped her—yes, I did actually worship her. I would have done anything she ordered me, except leave her alone; and that I wouldn't do. I dare say I might have got into a sort of friendship with her if she'd had any home, any relatives, any place to receive me in. But what can a girl do with nothing but a bed-sitting-room? I asked her to go up the river; I asked her to dinner and to lunch, and to bring her friends with her; I even asked her to go with me to an A.B.C. shop, but she wouldn't. She was quite right, in a general way. How could she guess I wasn't like the rest, or like what I had been?

Once, when she let me walk with her from Hugo's down to Walham Green, I nearly went mad with joy. I think I verily was mad for a time. I used to take out licenses for our marriage, and I used to buy clothes for her—heaps of clothes, in case. Yes, I was as good as mad then. And when she made it clear that this walking by my side was nothing at all, meant nothing, and must be construed as nothing, I grew still more mad.

At last I wrote to her that if she didn't call and see me at my flat, I should blow my brains out. I didn't expect her to call, and I did expect that I should blow my brains out. I was ready to do so. A year more or a year less on this earth—what did it matter to me?

Some people may think—*you* may think, Polycarp—that a man like me, under sentence of death from a doctor, had no right to make love to a woman. That may be so. But in love there isn't often any question of right. Human instincts have no regard for human justice, and when the instinct is strong enough, the sense of justice simply ceases to exist for it. When you're in love—enough—you don't argue. You desire—that's all.

To my amazement, she came to the flat. When she was announced, I could scarcely tell the servant to show her in, and when she entered, I couldn't speak at all for a moment. She was so—however, I won't describe her. I couldn't, for one thing. No one could describe that woman. She didn't make any fuss. She didn't cry out that she had ruined her reputation or anything like that. She simply said that she had received my letter, and that she had believed the sincerity of my threat, while regretting it, and what did I wish to say to her—she wouldn't be able to stay long. It goes without saying I couldn't begin. I couldn't frame a sentence. So I suggested we should have some tea. Accordingly, we had some tea. She poured it out, and we discussed the furniture of the drawing-room. I might have known she had fine taste in furniture. She had. When tea was over, she seemed to be getting a little impatient. Then I rang for the tray to be removed, and as soon as we were alone again, I started: 'Miss Payne—'

Now, when I started like that, I hadn't the ghost of a notion what I was going to say. And then the idea stepped into my head all of a sudden: 'Why not tell her exactly what your situation is? Why not be frank with her, and see how it works?' It was an inspiration. Though I didn't believe in it, and thought in a kind of despair that I was spoiling my chances, it was emphatically an inspiration, and I was obliged to obey it.

So I told her what Darcy had told me. I explained how it was that I couldn't live long. I said I had nothing to hope for in this world, no joy, nothing but blackness and horror. I said how tremendously I was in love with her. I said I knew she wasn't in love with me, but at the same time I thought she ought to have sufficient insight to see that I was fundamentally a decent chap. I went so far as to say that I didn't see how she could dislike me. And I said: 'I ask you to marry me. It will only be for a year or two, but that year or two are all my life, while only a fraction of yours. I am rich, and after my death you will be rich, and free from the necessity of this daily drudgery of yours. But I don't ask you to marry me for money; I ask you to marry me out of pity. I ask you, out of kindness to the most unfortunate and hopeless man in the world, to give me a trifle out of your existence. Merely out of pity; merely because it is a woman's part in the world to render pity and balm. I won't hide anything from you. There will be the unpleasant business of my sudden death, which will be a shock to you, even if you learn to hate me. But you would get over that. And you would always afterwards have the consciousness of having changed the last months of a man's career from hell to heaven. There's no disguising the fact that it's a strange proposition I'm making to you, but the proposition is not more strange than the situation. Will you consent, or won't you?' She was going to say something, but I stopped her. I said: 'Wait a moment. I shan't try to terrorize you by threats of suicide. And now, before you say "Yes" or "No," I give you my solemn word not to commit suicide if you say "No."' Then I went on in the same strain appealing to her pity, and telling her how humble I should be as a husband.

I could see I had moved her; and now I think over the scene I fancy that my appeal must have been a lot more touching than I imagined it was when I was making it.

She said: 'I have always liked you a little. But I haven't loved you, and I don't love you.' And then, after a pause—I was determined to say nothing more—she said: 'Yes, I will marry you. I may be doing wrong—I am certainly doing something very unusual; but I have no one to advise me against it, and I will follow my impulse and marry you. I needn't say that I shall do all I can to be a good wife to you. Ours will be a curious marriage.... Perhaps, after all, I am very wicked!'

I cried out: 'No, you aren't—no you aren't! The saints aren't in it with you!'

She smiled at this speech. She's so sensible, Camilla is. She's like a man in some things; all really great women are.

I could tell you a lot more that passed immediately afterwards, but I can feel already my voice is getting a bit tired. Besides, it's nothing to you, Polycarp.

Then, afterwards, I said: 'You *will* love me, you know.'

And I meant it. Any man in similar circumstances would have said it and meant it. She smiled again. And then I wanted to be alone with her, to enjoy the intimacy of her presence, without a lot of servants all over the place; so I went out of the drawing-room and packed off the whole tribe for the evening, all except Mrs. Dant. I kept Mrs. Dant to attend on Camilla.

We had dinner sent up; it was like a picnic, jolly and childish. Camilla was charming. And then I took photographs of her by flashlight, with immense success. We developed them together in the dark-room. That evening was the first time I had ever been really happy in all my life. And I was really happy, although every now and then the idea would shoot through my head: 'Only for a year or two at most; perhaps only for a day or two!'

I returned to the dark-room alone for something or other, and when I came back into the drawing-room she was not there. By heaven! my heart went into my mouth. I feared she had run away, after all. However, I met her in the passage. She looked very frightened; her face was quite changed; but she said nothing had occurred. I kissed her; she let me.

Soon afterwards she went on to the roof. She tried to be cheerful, but I saw she had something on her mind. She said she must go home, and begged my permission to precede me into the flat in order to prepare for her departure. I consented. When ten minutes had elapsed I followed, and in the drawing-room, instead of finding Camilla, I found Louis Ravengar.

I needn't describe my surprise at all that.

Ravengar was beside himself with rage. I gathered after a time that he claimed Camilla as his own. He said I had stolen her from him. I couldn't tell exactly what he was driving at, but I parleyed with him a little until I could get my revolver out of a drawer in my escritoire. He jumped at me. I thrust him back without firing, and we stood each of us ready for murder. I couldn't say how long that lasted. Suddenly he glanced across the room, and his eyes faltered, and I became aware that Camilla had entered silently. I was so startled at her appearance and by the transformation in Ravengar that I let off the revolver involuntarily. I heard Camilla order him, in a sharp, low voice, to leave instantly. He defied her for a second, and then went. Before leaving he stuttered, in a dreadful voice: 'I shall kill you'— meaning her. 'I may as well hang for one thing as for another.'

I said to Camilla, gasping: 'What is it all? What does it mean?'

She then told me, after confessing that she had caught Ravengar hiding in the dressing-room, and had actually suspected that I had been in league with him against her, that long ago she had by accident seen Ravengar commit a crime. She would not tell me what crime; she would give me no particulars. Still, I gathered that, if not actually murder, it was at least homicide. After that Ravengar had pestered her to marry him—had even said that he would be content with a purely formal marriage; had offered her enormous sums to agree to his proposal; and had been constantly repulsed by her. She admitted to me that he had appeared to be violently in love with her, but that his motive in wanting marriage was to prevent her from giving evidence against him. I asked her why she had not communicated with the police long since, and she replied that nothing would induce her to do that.

'But,' I said, 'he will do his best to kill you.'

She said: 'I know it.'

And she said it so solemnly that I became extremely frightened. I knew Ravengar, and I had marked the tone of his final words; and the more I pondered the more profoundly I was imbued with this one idea: 'The life of my future wife is not safe. Nothing can make it safe.'

I urged her to communicate with the police. She refused absolutely.

'Then one day you will be killed,' I said.

She gazed at me, and said: 'Can't you hit on some plan to keep me safe for a year?'

I demanded: 'Why a year?'

I thought she was thinking of my short shrift.

She said: 'Because in a year Mr. Ravengar will probably have—passed away.'

Not another word of explanation would she add.

'Yes,' I said; 'I can hit on a plan.'

And, as a matter of fact, a scheme had suddenly flashed into my head.

She asked me what the scheme was. And I murmured that it began with our marriage on the following day. I had in my possession a license which would enable us to go through the ceremony at once.

'Trust me,' I said. 'You have trusted me enough to agree to marry me. Trust me in everything.'

I did not venture to tell her just then what my scheme was.

She went to her lodging that night in my brougham. After she had gone I found poor old Mrs. Dant drugged in the kitchen. On the next morning Camilla and I were married at a registry office. She objected to the registry-office at first, but in the end she agreed, on the condition that I got her a spray of orange-blossom to wear at her breast. It's no business of yours, Polycarp, but I may tell you that this feminine trait, this almost childish weakness, in a woman of so superb and powerful a character, simply enchanted me. I obtained the orange-blossom.

Then you will remember I sent for you, Polycarp, made my will, and accompanied you to my safe in your private vault, in order to deposit there some secret instructions. I shall not soon forget your mystification, and how you chafed under my imperative commands.

Camilla and I departed to Paris, my brain full of my scheme, and full of happiness, too. We went to a private hotel to which Darcy had recommended us, suitable for honeymoons. The following morning I was, perhaps, inclined to smile a little at our terror of Ravengar; but, peeping out of the window early, I saw Ravengar himself standing on the pavement in the Rue St. Augustin.

I told Camilla I was going out, and that she must not leave that room, nor admit anyone into it, until I returned. I felt that Ravengar, what with disappointed love, and jealousy, and fear of the consequences of a past crime, had developed into a sort of monomaniac in respect to Camilla. I felt he was capable of anything. I should not have been surprised if he had hired a room opposite to us on the other side of that narrow street, and directed a fusillade upon Camilla.

When I reached the street he had disappeared—melted away.

It was quite early. However, I walked up the Rue de Grammont, and so to Darcy's, and I routed him out of bed. I gave him the entire history of the case. I convinced him of its desperateness, and I unfolded to him my scheme. At first he fought shy of it. He said it might ruin him. He said such things could not be done in London. I had meant to carry out the scheme in this flat. Hence the reason, Polycarp, of the clause in my will which provides for the sealing up of the flat in case I die within two months of my wedding. You see, I feared that I might be cut off before the plan was carried out or before all traces of it were cleared away, and I wanted to keep the place safe from prying eyes. As it happened, there was no need for such a precaution, as you will see, and I shall make a new will to-morrow.

Darcy said suddenly: 'Why not carry out your plan here in Paris; and now?'

The superior advantages of this alternative were instantly plain. It would be safer for Camilla, since it would operate at once; and also Darcy said that the formal details could be arranged much better in Paris than in London, as doctors could be found there who would sign anything, and clever sculptors, who did not mind a peculiar commission, were more easily obtainable in the Quartier Montparnasse than in the neighbourhood of the Six Bells and the Arts Club, Chelsea.

We found the doctor and the sculptor.

The hotel was informed that Camilla was ill, and that the symptom pointed to typhoid fever. Naturally, she kept her room. That day the sculptor, a young American, who said that a thing was 'bully' when he meant it was good, arrived, and took a mask of Camilla's head. By the way, this was a most tedious and annoying process. The two straws through which the poor girl had to breathe while her face was covered with that white stuff—! Oh, well, I needn't go into that.

The next day typhoid fever was definitely announced. Hotels generally prefer these things to be kept secret, but we published it everywhere—it was part of our plan. In a few hours the entire Rue St. Augustin was aware that the English bride recently arrived from London was down with typhoid fever.

The disease ran its course. Sometimes Camilla was better, sometimes worse. Then all of a sudden a hæmorrhage supervened, and the young wife died, and the young husband was stricken with trouble and grief. The whole street mourned. The death even got into the Paris dailies, and the correspondence column of the Paris edition of the *New York Herald* was filled with outcries against the impurities of Parisian water.

It was colossal. I laughed, Polycarp.

My mind unhinged by sorrow, I insisted on taking the corpse to London for burial. I had a peculiar affection for the Brompton Cemetery, though neither her ancestors nor mine had been buried there. I insisted on Darcy accompanying me. The procession left the Rue St. Augustin, and the hotel was disinfected. This alone cost me a thousand francs. I gave the sculptor one thousand five hundred, and the doctor two thousand. Then there were the expenses of the journey with the coffin. I forget the figure, but I know it was prodigious.

But I was content. For, of course, Camilla was not precisely in that coffin. Camilla had not been suffering from precisely typhoid fever. In strict fact, she had never been ill the least bit in the world. In strict fact, she had been spirited out of the hotel one night, and at the very moment when her remains were crossing the Channel in charge of an inconsolable widower, she was in the middle of the Mediterranean on a steamer. The coffin contained a really wonderful imitation of her outward form, modelled and coloured by the American sculptor in a composition consisting largely of wax. The widower's one grief was that he was forced to separate himself from his life's companion for a period of, at least, a week.

A pretty enough scheme, wasn't it, Polycarp? We shall shortly bury the wax effigy in Brompton Cemetery, with the assistance of Hugo's undertakers, and a parson or so, and grave-diggers, and registrars of deaths, and so on and so on. Louis Ravengar will breathe again, thankful that typhoid fever has relieved him of an unpleasant incubus, and since Camilla is underground, he will speedily forget all about her. She will be absolutely safe from him. The inconsolable widower will ostentatiously seek distraction in foreign travel, and in a fortnight, at most, will, under another name, resume his connubial career in a certain villa unsurpassed, I am told, for its picturesque situation.

To-morrow or the next day I must make that new will, dispensing with the shutting-up of the flat. The secret instructions, however, will stand.

You may wonder why I confide all this to the phonograph, Polycarp. I will tell you. The record will be placed by me to-morrow in my safe in your vault. To-night I shall lock it up in the safe here. When I am dead, Polycarp, you will find that the secret instructions instruct you to realize all my estate, and to keep the proceeds in negotiable form until a lady named Mrs. Catherine Pounds, a widow, comes to you with an autograph letter from me. You will hand everything to that lady, or to her representative, without any further inquiry. But it has struck me this very day, Polycarp, that you, with your confounded suspicious and legal nature, when you see Mrs. Catherine Pounds, if she should come in person, may recognise in her a striking resemblance to Camilla. And you may put difficulties in the way, and rake up history which was not meant to be raked up. This phonographic record is to prevent you from doing so, if by chance you have an impulse to do so. Think it over carefully, Polycarp. Consider our situation, and obey my instructions without a murmur. The thought of the false death certificates and burial certificates, and of the unprofessionalism of Darcy, will abrade your legal susceptibilities; but submit to the torture for my sake, Polycarp. You are human. I shall add to the letter which Mrs. Catherine Pounds will bring you a note to say that if you have any scruples, you are to listen to the phonographic records in the safe; if not, you are to destroy the phonographic records.

Do I seem gay, Polycarp?

I ought to be. I have carried through my scheme. I have outwitted Ravengar. I have saved Camilla from death at his hands. I can look forward to an idyll—brief, perhaps, but ecstatic—in a villa with the loveliest view on all the Mediterranean. I ought to be gay. And yet I am not. And it is not the knowledge of my fatal disease that saddens me. No; I think I have been saddened by a day and a night spent with that coffin. It is a fraud of a coffin, but it exists. And when I saw it just now occupying the drawing-room, it gave me a sudden shock. It somehow took hold of my imagination. I was obliged to look within, and to touch the waxen image there. And that image seemed unholy. I did not care to dwell on the thought of it going into the ground, with all the solemnities of the real thing. What do you suppose will happen to that waxen image on the Judgment Day, Polycarp? Surely, someone in authority, possibly a steward, fussy and overworked, will exclaim: 'There is some mistake here!' I can hear you say that I am mad, Polycarp, that Francis Tudor was always a little 'wrong.' But I am not mad. It is only that my brain is too agile, too fanciful. I am a great deal more sane than you, Polycarp.

And I am trying to put some heart into myself. I am trying to make ready to enjoy the brief ecstatic future where Camilla awaits me. But I am so tired, Polycarp. And there's no disguising the fact that it's an awful nuisance never to be quite sure whether you won't fall down dead the next minute or the next second. I must go in and have another glance at that singular swindle of a coffin.

The phonograph went off into an inarticulate whirr of its own machinery. The recital was over. Tudor must have died immediately after securing the record in the safe in his bedroom, where Hugo had just listened to it.

'She lives!' was Hugo's sole thought.

The profound and pathetic tragedy of Tudor's career did not touch him until long afterwards.

'She lives! Ravengar lives! Ravengar probably knows where she is, and I do not know! And Ravengar is at large! I have set him at large.'

His mind a battlefield on which the most glorious hope struggled against a frenzied fear, Hugo rose from the chair in front of the phonograph-stand, and, after a slight hesitation, left the flat as he had entered it. Before dawn the pane had been replaced in the drawing-room window, and the side-door secured.

PART III

THE TOMB

CHAPTER XX

'ARE YOU THERE?'

The next morning Hugo's dreams seemed to be concerned chiefly with a telephone, and the telephone-bell of his dreams made the dreams so noisy that even while asleep he knew that his rest was being outrageously disturbed. He tried to change the subject of his fantastic visions, but he could not, and the telephone-bell rang nearly all the time. This was the more annoying in that he had taken elaborate precautions to secure perfect repose. Perfect repose was what he needed after quitting Tudor's flat. He felt that he had stood as much as a man can expect himself to stand. In the vault, and again in the flat, his life had been in danger; he had suffered the ignominy of the ruined sale; he had come to grips with Ravengar, and let Ravengar go free; he had listened to the amazing recital of the phonograph. Moreover, between the interview with Ravengar and the burglary of the flat he had summoned his Council of Ten, or, rather, his Council of Nine (Bentley being absent, dead), had addressed all his employés, had separated three traitorous shopwalkers, ten traitorous cashiers, and forty-two traitorous servers from the main body, and sent them packing, had arranged for the rehabilitation of Lady Brice (*née* Kentucky-Webster), had appointed a new guardian to the Safe Deposit, had got on the track of the stolen stoles, and had approved special advertisements for every daily paper in London.

And, finally and supremely, he had experienced the greatest stroke of joy, ecstatic and bewildering joy, of his whole existence—the news that Camilla lived. It was this tremendous feeling of joy, and not by any means his complex and variegated worries, that might have prevented him from obtaining the sleep which Nature demanded.

On reaching the dome at 2 a.m., he had taken four tabloids, each containing $0·324$ gramme of trional, and had drunk the glass of hot milk which Simon always left him in case he should want it. And he had written on a sheet of paper the words: 'I am not to be disturbed before 10 a.m., no matter what happens; but call me at ten.—H.'; and had put the sheet of paper on Simon's door-mat. And then he had stumbled into bed, and abandoned himself to sleep—not without reluctance, for he did not care to lose, even for a few hours, the fine consciousness of that sheer joy. He desired to rush off instantly into the universe at large and discover Camilla, wherever she might be.

Of course, he had dreamed of Camilla, but the telephone-bell had drowned the remembered accents of her voice. The telephone-bell had silenced everything. The telephone-bell had grown from a dream into a nightmare; and at last he had said to himself in the nightmare: 'I might just as well be up and working as lying throttled here by this confounded nightmare.' And by an effort of will he had wakened. And even after he was roused, and had switched on the light, which showed the hands of the clock at a quarter to ten, he could still hear the telephone-bell of his nightmare. And then the truth occurred to him, as the truth does occur surprisingly to people whose sleep has been disturbed, that the telephone-bell was a real telephone-bell, and not in the least the telephone-bell of a dream, and it was ringing, ringing, ringing in the dome. There were fifteen lines of telephone in the Hugo building, and one of them ran to the dome. Few persons called him up on it, because few persons knew its precise number, but he used it considerably himself.

'Anyhow,' he murmured, 'I've had over seven and a half hours' sleep, and that's something.'

And as he got out of bed to go across to the telephone, his great joy resumed possession of him, and he was rather glad than otherwise that the telephone had forced him to wake.

'Well, well, well?' he cried comically, lifting the ear-piece off the hook and stopping the bell.

'Are you there?' the still small voice of the telephone whispered in his ear.

'I should think I was here!' he cried. 'Who are you?'

'Are you Mr. Hugo?' asked the voice.

'I'm what's left of Mr. Hugo,' he answered in a sort of drunken tone. The power of the sedative was still upon him. 'Who are you? You've pretty nearly rung my head off.'

'I just want to say good-bye to you,' said the voice.

'What!'

Hugo started, glancing round the vast room, which was in shadow except where a solitary light threw its yellow glare on the dial of the clock.

'Are you there?' asked the voice patiently once again.

'It isn't'—something prompted him to use a Christian name—'it isn't Louis?'

'Yes.'

'Where are you, then?' Hugo demanded.

'Not far off,' replied the mysterious voice in the telephone.

It was unmistakably the voice of Louis Ravengar, but apparently touched with some new quality, some quality of resigned and dignified despair. Hugo wondered where the man could be. And the sinister magic of the telephone, which brought this sad, quiet voice to him from somewhere out of the immensity of England, but which would not yield up the secret of its hiding, struck him strangely.

'Are you there?' said the voice yet again.

'Yes.'

Hugo shivered, but whether it was from cold—he wore nothing but his pyjamas—or from apprehension he could not decide.

'I'm saying good-bye,' said the voice once more. 'I suppose you mean to have the police after me, and so I mean to get out of their way. See? But first I wished to tell you—*crrrck cluck*—Eh? What?'

'I didn't speak.'

'It's these Exchange hussies, then. I wanted to tell you I've thought a lot about our interview last night. What you said was true enough, Owen. I admit that, and so I am going to end it. Eh? Are you there? That girl keeps putting me off.'

'End what?'

'End *it—it—it*! I'm not making anybody happy, not even myself, and so I'm going to end it. But I'll tell you her address first. I know it.'

'Whose address?'

'Hers—Camilla's. If I tell you, will you promise not to say a word about me speaking to you on the telephone this morning?'

'Yes.'

'Not a word under any circumstances?'

'Certainly.'

'Well, it's 17, Place Saint-Étienne, Bruges, Belgium.'

'17, Place Saint-Étienne, Bruges. That's all right. I shan't forget. Look here, Louis, you'd better clear out of England. Go to America. Do you hear? I don't understand this about "ending it." You surely aren't thinking of—'

He felt quite magnanimous towards Ravengar. And he was aware that he could get to Bruges in six hours or so.

'That idea of yours about chloroform,' said the voice, 'and going into the vault, and being shut up there, is a very good one. Nobody would know, except the person whom one paid to shut the door after one.'

'I say, where are you?' Hugo asked curtly. He was at a loss how to treat these singular confidences.

'And so is that idea good about merely ending one incarnation and beginning another. That's much better than calling it death.'

'I shall ring you off,' said Hugo.

'Wait a moment,' said the voice, still patiently. 'If you should hear the name Callear—'

There was a pause.

'Well?' Hugo inquired, 'what name?'

'Callear—C-a-l-l-e-a-r. If you should hear that name soon—'

'What then?'

'Remember your promise of secrecy—that's all. Good-bye.'

'I wish you'd tell me where you are.'

'Not far off,' said the voice. 'I shall never be far off, I think. When you've found Camilla and brought her here'—the tone of the voice changed and grew almost malignant despite its reticence—'you'd like to know that I was always near to, somewhere underneath, mouldering, wouldn't you?'

'What did you say?'

'I said mouldering. Good-bye.'

'But look here—'

The bell rang off. Louis Ravengar had finished his good-bye. Hugo tried in vain to resume communication with him. He could not even get any sort of reply from the Exchange.

'It's a queer world,' he soliloquized, as he returned to bed. 'What does the man mean?'

He was still happy in the prospect of finding Camilla, but it was as though his happiness were a pool in a private ground, and some trespasser had troubled it with a stone.

The clock struck ten, and Simon entered with tea and the paper.

CHAPTER XXI

SUICIDE

The paper contained a whole-page advertisement of Hugo's great annual sale, and also a special half-page advertisement headed 'Hugo's Apology and Promise'—a message to the public asking pardon of the public for the confusion, inconvenience, and disappointments of the previous day, hinting that the mystery of the affair would probably be elucidated in a criminal court, and stating that a prodigious number of silvered fox-stoles would positively be available from nine o'clock that morning at a price even lower than the figure named in the original announcement. The message further stated that a special Complaint Office had been opened as a branch of the Inquiry Bureau, and that all complaints by customers who had suffered on New Year's Day would there be promptly and handsomely dealt with.

In addition to Hugo's advertisements, there were several columns of news describing the singular phenomena of the sale, concluding with what a facetious reporter had entitled 'Interviews with Survivors.'

As he read the detailed accounts Hugo knew, perhaps for the first time in his life, what it was 'to go hot and cold all over.' However, he was decidedly inclined to be optimistic.

'Anyhow,' he said, 'it's the best ad. I ever had. Still, it's a mercy there were no deaths.'

He began to dress hurriedly, furiously. Already the second day of the sale had been in progress for more than an hour, and he had not even visited the scene of the campaign. Simon had said nothing; it was not Simon's habit to speak till he was spoken to. And Hugo did not feel inclined to ask questions; he preferred to reconnoitre in person. Yes, he would descend instantly, and afterwards, when he had satisfied himself that the evil had been repaired, he would consider about Camilla.... By neglecting all else, he could reach her in time for dinner.... Should he?... (At this point he plunged into his cold bath.) ... No! He was Hugo before he was Camilla's lover. He would be a tradesman for yet another ten hours. He had a duty to London....

Then Ravengar wandered into his thoughts and confused them.

Just as he was assuming his waistcoat, Simon entered.

'Mr. Galpin, sir.'

'And who the d---l is Mr. Galpin?' asked Hugo.

'Mr. Galpin is the gentleman who saved your life yesterday, sir,' said Simon with admirable sangfroid. 'He has called for a hundred pounds.'

'Show him in here immediately,' said Hugo.

Mr. Galpin appeared in the dressing-room, looking more than ever like an extremely successful commercial traveller. Hugo could not think of any introductory remark worthy of the occasion.

'I needn't say how grateful I am,' Hugo began.

'Certainly you needn't,' said Mr. Galpin. 'I understand. I've been under lock and key myself.'

'I should offer you more than this paltry sum,' said Hugo, with a smile, 'but I know, of course, that a man like you can always obtain all the money he really wants.'

Mr. Galpin smiled, too.

'However,' continued Hugo, detaching his watch from his waistcoat, 'I will ask you to take something that you can't get elsewhere. This is the thinnest watch in the world. Bréguet, of the Rue de la Paix, Paris, made it specially for me. It is exactly the same size as a five-shilling piece. It repeats the quarters, shows the time in four cities, and does practically everything except tell the weather and the political party in power. It has one drawback. Only Bréguet can clean it, and he will charge you five guineas for the job, besides probably having you arrested for unlawful possession. I must write to him. Such as it is, accept it.'

The golden, jewelled toy was offered and received with a bow. The practised hands of Mr. Galpin had opened the case in two seconds.

'How do you regulate it?' demanded Mr. Galpin, staring at the movement.

'You don't,' said Hugo proudly; 'it never needs it.'

Mr. Galpin stood corrected.

'If there's anything in my line I can do for you at any time, sir,' said he.

Hugo pondered.

Mr. Galpin put the watch in his waistcoat-pocket, and, tearing the hundred-pound note in two halves, placed one half in the left breast pocket of his coat, and the other half in the right breast pocket of his coat.

'Could you have opened that vault,' Hugo asked, 'if both keys had been lost?'

'No, sir, I could not. It's such people as you who are ruining my profession, sir.'

'You think the vault is impregnable?'

'Yes, sir,' said Mr. Galpin. 'I should say its name was just about as near being Gibraltar as makes no matter.'

'I was only wondering,' Hugo mused aloud, 'only wondering.... Ah, well, I won't trouble you with my fancies.'

'As you wish, sir. Good-bye.'

'Good-bye, Mr. Galpin. And thank you!'

'Thank *you*, sir,' said Mr. Galpin, and disappeared.

'Simon,' Hugo ordered immediately afterwards, handing Simon the token, 'run down and get me the best gold watch in the place.'

Throughout the morning Hugo's thoughts were far away. Most frequently they were in Belgium, but now and then they paid a strange incomprehensible visit with Ravengar to the vault.

While he was lunching under the dome, Albert Shawn came in with the early edition of the *Evening Herald*, containing a prominent item headed, 'Feared Suicide of Mr. Louis Ravengar.' The paper stated that Mr. Ravengar had gone to Dover on the previous evening, had been seen to board the Calais steamer, and had been missed soon after the boat had left the harbour. His hat, umbrella, rug, and bag had been found on deck. As the night was quite calm, there could be no other explanation than that of suicide. The *Evening Herald* gave a sympathetic biography of Mr. Ravengar ('one of our proprietors'), and attributed his suicide to a fit of depression caused by the entirely groundless rumours which had circulated during the late afternoon connecting him with the scandalous disturbances at Hugo's sale.

Hugo dropped the organ of public opinion.

'H'm!' he observed to Albert.

'I'm not surprised, sir,' said Albert.

'Aren't you?' said Hugo. 'Then, there's nothing more to be said.'

Since Louis Ravengar had certainly been talking with Hugo that selfsame morning, it was obviously impossible that he should have committed suicide in the English Channel some twelve hours earlier. Why, then, had he arranged for this elaborate deception to be practised? What was his scheme? His voice through the telephone had been so quiet, so resigned, so pathetic; only towards the end had it become malevolent.

Hugo perceived that he must go down to the vault. No! He dared not go himself. The sight of that vault, after yesterday's emotions, would surely be beyond his power to bear!

'Albert,' he said, 'go to the Safe Deposit.'

'Yes, sir.'

'And inquire if anyone named—'

Hugo stopped.

'Named what, sir?'

'Never mind. I'll go myself. By the way,' he said, 'I must run over to Belgium to-night. Perhaps I may take you with me.'

'Don't forget the inquest on Bentley to-morrow, sir. You'll have to attend that.'

Hugo made a gesture of excessive annoyance. He had forgotten the inquest.

'Take this telegram,' he said, suddenly inspired; and he scribbled out the following words: 'Darcy, 16, Boulevard des Italiens, Paris. Please come instantly; urgent case.—HUGO, London.'

'At any rate, I've made a beginning,' he murmured when Albert had gone. 'I can find out all that is to be known about Camilla from Darcy—if he comes. I wonder if he'll come. He'd better.'

And then, collecting his powers of self-control, he went slowly down to the Safe Deposit, and entered those steely and dreadful portals.

'Getting on all right?' he said to the newly-installed manager, a young man with light hair from the counting-house.

'Oh yes, Mr. Hugo.'

'Any new customers?'

He trembled for the reply.

'Yes, sir. Two gentlemen came as soon as we opened this morning, and took Vault 39. They paid a year's rent in advance. Two hundred pounds.'

'What did they want a whole vault for?'

'I can't say, sir. There was a lot of going to and fro with parcels and things, sir, and a lot of telephoning in the waiting-room. And one of them asked for a glass and some water. They were here a long time, sir.'

'When did they go?'

'It was about ten-thirty, sir, when one of the two gentlemen called me to bring my key and lock up the vault. The vault was properly locked, first with his key, and then with mine, and then he left. Perhaps it might be a quarter to eleven, sir.'

'But the other gentleman?'

'Oh, he must have slipped off earlier, sir. I didn't see him go.'

'What did he look like?'

'Oldish man, Mr. Hugo. Gray.'

The manager was somewhat mystified by this cross-examination.

'And the name?'

'The name? Let me see. Callear. Yes, Callear, sir.'

'What?'

'C-a-l-l-e-a-r.'

'What was the address?'

'Hotel Cecil. He said he would send a permanent address in a day or two.'

In half an hour Hugo had ascertained that no person named Callear was staying at the Hotel Cecil.

He understood now, understood too clearly, the meanings of Ravengar's strange utterances on the telephone. The man had determined to commit suicide, and he had chosen a way which was calculated with the most appalling ingenuity to ruin, if anything would ruin, Hugo's peace of mind for years to come—perhaps for ever. For the world, Ravengar was drowned. But Hugo knew that his body was lying in that vault.

'Louis had an accomplice,' Hugo reflected. 'Who can that have been? Who could have been willing to play so terrible a rôle?'

CHAPTER XXII

DARCY

That night, when he was just writing out some cheques in aid of charities conducted by Lady Brice (*née* Kentucky-Webster), Simon entered with a card. The hour was past eleven.

Hugo read on the card, 'Docteur Darcy.'

He had nearly forgotten that he had sent for Darcy; in fact, he was no longer quite sure why he had sent for him, since he meant, in any case, to hasten to Belgium at the earliest moment.

'You are exceedingly prompt, doctor,' he said, when Darcy came into the dome. 'I thank you.'

The cosmopolitan physician appeared to be wearing the same tourist suit that he had worn on the night of Tudor's death. The sallowness of his impassive face had increased somewhat, and his long thin hands had their old lackadaisical air. 'You don't look at all the man for such a part,' said Hugo in the privacy of his brain, 'but you played your part devilish well that night, my pale friend. You deceived me perfectly.'

'Prompt?' smiled the doctor, shaking hands, and removing his overcoat with fatigued gestures.

'Yes; you must have caught the 4 p.m. express, and come via Folkstone and Boulogne.'

'I did,' said Darcy.

'And yet I expect you didn't get my telegram till after two o'clock.'

'I have received no telegram from you, my dear Mr. Hugo. It had not arrived when I left.'

'Then your presence here to-night is due to a coincidence merely?'

'Not at all,' said Darcy; 'it is due to an extreme desire on my part to talk to you.'

'The desire is mutual,' Hugo answered, gently insisting that Darcy should put away his cigarettes and take a Muria. 'Dare I ask—'

Darcy had become suddenly nervous, and he burst out, interrupting Hugo:

'The suicide of Mr. Ravengar was in this morning's Paris papers. And I may tell you at once that it's in connection with that affair that I'm here.'

'I also—' Hugo began.

'I may tell you at once,' Darcy proceeded with increasing self-consciousness, 'that when I had the pleasure of meeting you before, Mr. Hugo, I was forced by circumstances, and by my promise to a dead friend, to behave in a manner which was very distasteful to me. I was obliged to lie to you, to play a trick on you—in short—well, I can only ask you for your sympathy. I have a kind of a forlorn notion that you'll understand—after I've explained, as I mean to do—'

'If you refer to the pretended death of Tudor's wife—' said Hugo.

'Then you know?' Darcy cried, astounded.

'I know. I know everything, or nearly everything.'

'How?' Darcy retreated towards the piano.

'I will explain how some other time,' Hugo replied, going also to the piano and facing his guest. 'You did magnificently that night, doctor. Don't imagine for a moment that my feelings towards you in regard to that disastrous evening are anything but those of admiration. And now tell me about her—about *her*. She is well?'

Hugo put a hand on the man's shoulder, and persuaded him back to his chair.

'She is well—I hope and believe,' answered Darcy.

'You don't see her often?'

'On the contrary, I see her every day, nearly.'

'But if she lives at Bruges and you are in Paris—'

'Bruges?'

'Yes; Place Saint-Étienne.'

Darcy thought for a second.

'So it's *you* who have been on the track,' he murmured.

Hugo, too, became meditative in his turn.

'I wish you would tell me all that happened since—since that night,' he said at length.

'I ask nothing better,' said Darcy. 'Since Ravengar is dead and all danger passed, there is no reason why you should not know everything that is to be known. Well, Mr. Hugo, I have had an infinity of trouble with that girl.'

Hugo's expression gave pause to the doctor.

'I mean with Mrs. Tudor,' he added correctively. 'I'll begin at the beginning. After the disappearance—the typhoid disappearance, you know—she went to Algiers. Tudor had taken a villa at Mustapha Supérieure, the healthiest suburb of the town. After Tudor's sudden death I telegraphed to her to come back to me in Paris. I couldn't bring myself to wire that Tudor was dead. I only said he was ill. And at first she wouldn't come. She thought it was a ruse of Ravengar's. She thought Ravengar had discovered her hiding-place, and all sorts of things. However, in the end she came. I met her at Marseilles. You wouldn't believe, Mr. Hugo, how shocked she was by the news of her husband's death. Possibly I didn't break it to her too neatly. She didn't pretend to love him—never had done—but she was shocked all the same. I had a terrible scene with her at the Hotel Terminus at Marseilles. Her whole attitude towards the marriage changed completely. She insisted that it was plain to her then that she had simply sold herself for money. She said she hated herself. And she swore she would never touch a cent of Tudor's fortune—not even if the fortune went to the Crown in default of legal representatives.'

'Poor creature!' Hugo breathed.

'However,' Darcy proceeded, 'something had to be done. She was supposed to be dead, and if her life was to be saved from Ravengar's vengeance, she just had to continue to be dead—at any rate, as regards England. So she couldn't go back to England. Now I must explain that my friend Tudor hadn't left her with much money.'

'That was careless.'

'It was,' Darcy admitted. 'Still, he naturally relied on me in case of necessity. And quite rightly. I was prepared to let Mrs. Tudor have all the money she wanted, she repaying me as soon as events allowed her to handle Tudor's estate. But as she had decided never to handle Tudor's estate, she had no prospect of being able to repay me. Hence she would accept nothing. Hence she began to starve. Awkward, wasn't it?'

'I see clearly that she could not come to England to earn her living,' said Hugo, 'but could she not have earned it in Paris?'

'No,' Darcy replied; 'she couldn't earn it regularly. And the reason was that she was too beautiful. Situation after situation was made impossible for her. She might easily have married in Paris, but earn her living there—no! In the end she was obliged to accept money from me, but only in very small sums, such as she could repay without much difficulty when Ravengar's death should permit her to return to England. She was always sure of Ravengar's death, but she would never tell me why. And now he's dead.'

'And there is no further obstacle to her coming to England?'

'None whatever. That is to say—except one.'

'What do you mean?' Hugo demanded.

Darcy had flushed.

'I'm in a very delicate position,' said Darcy. 'I've got to explain to you something that a man can't explain without looking an ass. The fact is—of course, you see, Mr. Hugo, I did all I could for her all the time. Not out of any special regard for her, but for Tudor's sake, you understand. She's awfully beautiful, and all that. I've nothing against her. But I believe I told you last year that I had been in love once. That "once" was enough. I've done with women, Mr. Hugo.'

'But how does this affect—' Hugo began to inquire, rather inimically.

'Can't you see? She doesn't *want* to leave Paris. I did all I could for her all the time. I've been her friend in adversity, and so on, and so on, and she's—she's—'

'What on earth are you driving at, man?'

'She's fallen in love with me. That's what I'm driving at. And now you know.'

'My dear sir,' said Hugo earnestly, 'if she is in love with you, you must marry her and make her happy.'

He did not desire to say this, but some instinct within him compelled him to utter the words.

'You told me that you loved her,' Darcy retorted.

'I told you the truth. I do.'

A silence ensued. All Hugo's previous discouragements, sadnesses, preoccupations, despairs, were as nothing in comparison with the black mood which came upon him when he learnt this simple fact—that Camilla had fallen in love with Darcy.

'She is still in Paris?' he asked, to end the silence.

'I—I don't know. I called at her lodgings at noon, and she had gone and left no address.'

Hugo jumped up.

'She can't have disappeared again?'

'Oh no; rest assured. Doubtless a mere change of rooms. When I return I shall certainly find a letter awaiting me.'

'Why did you come to me?'

'Well,' Darcy said, 'you told me you loved her, and I thought—I thought perhaps you'd come over to Paris, and see—see what could be done. That's why I came. The thing's on my mind, you know.'

'Just so,' Hugo answered, 'and I will come.'

CHAPTER XXIII

FIRST TRIUMPH OF SIMON

A week later, Simon and Albert stood talking together in Simon's room adjoining the dome. Simon had that air of absolute spruceness and freshness which in persons who have stayed at home is so extremely offensive to persons who have just arrived exhausted and unclean from a tiresome journey. It was Albert who, with Hugo, had arrived from the journey.

'Had a good time, Alb?' Simon asked.

'So-so,' said Albert cautiously.

'By the way, what did you go to Paris *for*?'

'Didn't you know?'

'How should I know, my son?'

'The governor wanted to find that girl of his.'

'What girl?' Simon asked innocently.

'Oh, chuck it, Si!' Albert remonstrated against these affectations of ignorance in a relative from whom he had no secrets.

'You mean Mrs. Tudor?'

'Yes.'

'She's disappeared again, has she? And you couldn't find her?'

Albert concurred.

'It seems to me, Alb,' said Simon, 'that you aren't shining very brilliantly just now as a detective. And I'm rather surprised, because I've been doing a bit of detective work myself, and it's nothing but just using your eyes.'

'What have you been up to?' Albert inquired.

'Oh, nothing. Never you mind. It's purely unofficial. You see, I'm not a detective. I'm only a servant that gets left at home. I've only been amusing myself. Still, I've found out a thing or two that you'd give your eyes to know, my son.'

'What?'

Albert pursued his quest of knowledge.

'You get along home to your little wife,' Simon enjoined him. 'You're a professional detective, you are. No doubt when you've recovered from Paris, and got into your stride, you'll find out all that I know and a bit over in about two seconds. Off you go!'

Simon's eyes glinted.

And later, when he was giving Hugo the last ministrations for the night, Simon looked at his lord as a cat looks at the mouse it is playing with—humorously, viciously, sarcastically.

'I'll give him a night to lie awake in,' said Simon's eyes.

But he only allowed his eyes to make this speech while Hugo's back was turned.

The next morning Hugo's mood was desolating. To speak to him was to play with fire. Obviously, Hugo had heard the clock strike all the hours. Nevertheless, Simon permitted himself to be blithe, even offensively blithe. And when Hugo had finished with him he ventured to linger.

'You needn't wait,' said Hugo, in a voice of sulphuric acid.

'So you didn't find Mrs. Francis Tudor, sir?' responded Simon, with calm and beautiful insolence.

It was insolence because, though few of Hugo's secrets were hid from Simon, the intercourse between master and servant was conducted on the basis of a convention that Simon's ignorance of Hugo's affairs was complete. And if the convention was ignored, as it sometimes was, Hugo alone had the right to begin the ignoring of it.

'What's that you said?' Hugo demanded.

'You didn't find Mrs. Francis Tudor, sir?' Simon blandly repeated.

'Mind your own business, my friend,' he said.

'Certainly, sir,' said Simon. 'But I had intended to add that possibly you had not been searching for Mrs. Tudor in the right city.'

Hugo stared at Simon, who retreated to the door.

'What in thunder do you mean?' Hugo asked coldly and deliberately.

At last Simon felt a tremor.

'I mean, sir, that I think I know where she is. At least, I know where she will be in a couple of hours' time.'

'Where?'

'In Department 42—her old department, sir.'

By a terrific effort Hugo kept calm.

'Simon,' he said, 'don't play any tricks on me. If you do, I'll thrash you first, and then dismiss you on the spot.'

'It's through the new manager of the drapery, sir, in place of Mr. Bentley—I forget his name. Mr. Bentley's room being all upset with police and accountants and things, the new manager has been using your office. And I was in there to-day, and he was engaging a young lady for the millinery, sir. He didn't recognise her, not having been here long enough, but I did. It was Miss Payne.'

'Impossible!'

'Yes, sir; Miss Payne—that is to say, Mrs. Tudor. I heard him say, "Very well, you can start to-morrow morning."'

'That's *this* morning?'

'Yes, sir.'

'Why didn't you tell me this last night?' Hugo roared.

'It slipped my memory, sir,' said Simon, surpassing all previous feats of insolence.

Hugo, speechless, waved him out of the room.

CHAPTER XXIV

THE LODGING-HOUSE

The thought of soon seeing her intoxicated him. His head swam, his heart leapt, his limbs did what they liked, being forgotten. And then, as he sobered himself, he tried seriously to find an answer to this question: Why had she returned, as it were surreptitiously, to the very building from which her funeral was supposed to have taken place? Could she imagine that oblivion had covered her adventure, and that the three thousand five hundred would ignore the fact that she was understood to be dead? He found no answer—at least, no satisfactory answer—except that women are women, and therefore incalculable.

'Go and see if she is there,' he said to Simon at five minutes to nine.

'She is there,' said Simon at five minutes past nine; 'in one of the work-rooms alone.'

Then Hugo put a heavy curb on his instincts, and came to a sudden resolve.

'Tell the new drapery manager,' he instructed Simon, 'to give instructions to Mrs. Tudor, or Miss Payne, whichever she calls herself, that she is to meet him in my central office at six o'clock this evening. He, however, is not to be there. She is to wait in the room alone, if I have not arrived. Inform no one that I have returned from Paris. I am now going out for the day.'

'Yes, sir.'

Hugo thereupon took train to Ealing. He walked circuitously through the middle of the day from Ealing to Harrow, alone with his thoughts in the frosty landscape. From Harrow he travelled by express to Euston, reaching town at five-thirty. Somehow or other the day had passed. He got to Sloane Street at six, and ascended direct to his central office.

Had his orders been executed? Would she be waiting? As he hesitated outside the door he was conscious that his whole frame shook. He entered silently.

Yes, she was there. She sat on the edge of a chair near the fire, staring at the fire. She was dressed in the customary black. Ah! it was the very face he had seen in the coffin, the same marvellous and incomparable features; not even sadder, not aged by a day; the same!

She turned at the sound of the closing of the door, and, upon seeing him, started slightly. Then she rose, and delicately blushed.

'Good-evening, Mr. Hugo,' she said, in a low, calm voice. 'I did not expect to see you.'

Great poetical phrases should have rushed to his lips—phrases meet for a tremendous occasion. But they did not. He sighed. 'I can only say what comes into my head,' he thought ruefully. And he said:

'Did I startle you?'

'Not much,' she replied. 'I knew I must meet you one day or another soon. And it is better at once.'

'Just so,' he said. 'It *is* better at once. Sit down, please. I've been walking all day, and I can scarcely stand.' And he dropped into a chair. 'Do you know, dear lady,' he proceeded, 'that Doctor Darcy and I have been hunting for you all over Paris?'

He managed to get a little jocularity into his tone, and this achievement eased his attitude.

'No,' she said, 'I didn't know. I'm very sorry.'

'But why didn't you let Darcy know that you were coming to London?'

'Mr. Hugo,' she answered, with a charming gesture, 'I will tell you.' And she got up from her chair and came to another one nearer his own. This delicious action filled him with profound bliss. 'When I read in the paper that Mr. Ravengar had committed suicide, I had just enough money in my pocket to pay my expenses to London, and to keep me a few days here. And I did so want to come! I did so want to come! I came by the morning train. It was an inspiration. I waited for nothing. I meant to write to Mr. Darcy that same night, but that same night I caught sight of him here in Sloane Street, so I knew it was no use writing just then. And I didn't care for him to see me. I thought I would give him time to return. As a matter of fact, I wrote yesterday evening. He would get the letter to-night. I hope my disappearance didn't cause you any anxiety?'

'Anxiety!' He repeated the word. 'You don't know what I've been through. I feared that Ravengar, before killing himself, had arranged to—to—I don't know what I feared. Horrible, unmentionable things! You can't guess what I've been through.'

'I, too, have suffered since we met last,' said Camilla softly.

'Don't talk of it—don't talk of it!' he entreated her. 'I know all. I saw your image in a coffin. I have heard your late husband's statement. And Darcy has told me much. Let us forget all that, and let us forget it for evermore. But you have to remember, nevertheless, that in London you have the reputation of being dead.'

'I have not forgotten,' she said, with a beautiful inflection and a bending of the head, 'that I promised to thank you the next time we met for what you did for me. Let me thank you now. Tell me how I can thank you!'

He wanted to cry out that she was divine, and that she must do exactly what she liked with him. And then he wanted to take her and clasp her till she begged for her breath. And he was tempted to inform her that though she loved Darcy as man was never loved before, still she should marry him, Hugo, or Darcy should die.

'Sit down,' he said in a quiet, familiar voice. 'Don't bother about thanking me. Just tell me all about the history of your relations with Ravengar.' And to himself he said: 'She shall talk to me, and I will listen, and we shall begin to be intimate. This is the greatest happiness I can have. Hang the future! I will give way to my mood. Darcy said she didn't want to leave Paris, but she has left it. That's something.'

'I will do anything you want,' she answered almost gaily; and she sat down again.

'I doubt it,' he smiled. 'However—'

The sense of intimacy, of nearness, gave him acute pleasure, as at their first interview months ago.

'I would *like* to tell you,' she began; 'and there is no harm now. Where shall I start? Well'—she became suddenly grave—'Mr. Ravengar used to pass my father's shop in the Edgware Road. He came in to buy things. It was a milliner's shop, and so he could buy nothing but bonnets and hats. He bought bonnets and hats. I often served him. He gave my father some very good hints about shares, but my father never took them. When my parents both died, Mr. Ravengar was extremely sympathetic, and offered me a situation in his office. I took it. I became his secretary. He was always very polite and considerate to me, except sometimes when he got angry with everybody, including me. He couldn't help being rude then. He had an old clerk named Powitt, who sat in the outer office, and seemed to do nothing. Powitt had just brains enough to gamble, and he gambled in the shares of Mr. Ravengar's companies. I know he lost money, because he used to confide in me and grumble at Mr. Ravengar for not giving him proper tips. Mr. Ravengar simply sneered at him—he was very hard. Powitt had a younger brother, who was engaged in another City office, and this younger brother also gambled in Ravengar shares, and also lost. The two brothers gambled more and more, and old Powitt once told me that Mr. Ravengar misled them sometimes from sheer—what shall I call it?'

'Devilry,' Hugo suggested. 'I can believe it. That would be his idea of a good joke.'

'By-and-by I learnt that they were in serious difficulties. Young Powitt was married, but his wife left him—I believe he had taken to drink. There was a glass partition between my room and Mr. Ravengar's—ground glass at the bottom, clear glass at the top. One night, after hours, I went back to the office for an umbrella which I had forgotten, and I found young Powitt trying to open the petty-cash-box in my room. He had not succeeded, and I just told him to go, and that I should forget I had seen him there. He kissed my hand. And just then the outer door of the office opened, and someone entered. I turned off the light in my room. Young Powitt crouched down. It was Mr. Ravengar. He went to his own room. I jumped on a chair, and looked through the glass screen. Old Powitt was hanging by the neck from the brass curtain-rod in Mr. Ravengar's room. While young Powitt was trying to get out of their difficulties by thieving, old Powitt had taken a shorter way. Mr. Ravengar looked at the body swinging there, and I heard him say, "Ah!" Like that!'

'Great heaven!' cried Hugo, 'you've been through sufficient in your time!'

'Yes.' Camilla paused. 'Mr. Ravengar cut down the body, searched the pockets, took out a paper, read it, and put it in his own pocket. Then the old man's lips twitched. He was not quite dead, after all. Mr. Ravengar stared at the face; and then, by means of putting a chair on a table and lifting Powitt on to the chair, he tied up the cord which he had cut, and left the poor old man to swing again. It was an—an interrupted suicide.'

She stopped once more, and Hugo fervently wished he had never asked her to begin. He gazed at her set face with a fascinated glance.

'All this time,' she resumed, 'young Powitt had been crouching on the floor, and had seen nothing.'

'And what did you do?'

'I fainted, and fell off my chair. The noise startled Mr. Ravengar, and he came round into my room. Young Powitt met him at the door, and, to explain his presence there, he said that he had come to see his brother. Mr. Ravengar said: "Your brother is in the next room." But instead of going into the next room, young Powitt ran off. Then Mr. Ravengar perceived me on the floor. My first words to him when I recovered consciousness were: "Why did you hang him up again, Mr. Ravengar?" He was staggered. He actually tried to justify himself, and said it was best for the old man—the old man had wanted to die, and so on. Mr. Ravengar certainly thought that young Powitt had seen what I had seen. That very night young Powitt was arrested for another theft, from his own employers, and it was not till after his arrest that he learnt that his brother had committed suicide. He got four years. When he received sentence, he swore that he would kill Mr. Ravengar immediately he came out of prison. I heard his threat. I knew him, and I knew that he meant it. He argued that Mr. Ravengar's financial operations had ruined thousands of people, including his brother and himself.

'But the inquest on old Powitt—I seem to remember about it. Why didn't you give evidence?'

'Because I was ill with brain-fever. When I recovered, all was finished. What was I to do? I warned Mr. Ravengar that young Powitt meant to kill him. He laughed. Of course, I left him. It is my belief that Mr. Ravengar was always a little mad. If he was not so before, this affair had strained his intelligence too much.'

'You did a very wrong thing,' said Hugo, 'in keeping silence.'

'Put yourself in my place,' Camilla answered. 'Think of all the facts. It was all so queer, And—and—Mr. Ravengar had found me in the room with young Powitt. Suppose he had—'

'Say no more,' Hugo besought her. 'How long is this ago?'

'Three years last June. In six months young Powitt's sentence will be up.'

Hugo nearly leapt from his chair.

'Is it possible, Mrs. Tudor,' he asked her eagerly, 'that you are not aware that in actual practice a reasonably well-behaved prisoner never serves the full period of his sentence? Marks for good conduct are allowed, and each mark means so many days deducted from the term.'

'I didn't know,' said Camilla simply. 'How should I know a thing like that?'

'I have no doubt that young Powitt is already free. And if he is—'

'You think that Mr. Ravengar's suicide may not have been a suicide?'

Hugo hesitated.

'Yes,' he said, and lapsed into reflection.

'I shall see you home,' he said.

'I am going to walk,' she replied. 'And I have to get my things from the cloak-room.'

'I will walk with you,' he said.

'What style the woman has!' he thought, enraptured.

They proceeded southwards in silence. Then suddenly she asked how he had left Mr. Darcy, and they began to talk about Darcy and Paris. Hugo encouraged her. He wished to know the worst.

'Except my father,' she said, 'I have never met anyone with more sense than Mr. Darcy, or anyone more kind. I might have been dead now if it hadn't been for Mr. Darcy.'

'Mr. Darcy is a very decent fellow,' Hugo remarked experimentally.

She turned and gave him a look. No, it was not a look; it was the merest fraction of a look, but it withered him up.

'She loves him!' he thought. 'And what's more, if she hadn't made up her mind to marry him, she wouldn't be so precious easy and facile and friendly with me. I might have guessed that.'

They passed Victoria Station, and came into Horseferry Road. She had informed him that she had taken a furnished room in Horseferry Road. The high and sinister houses appeared unspeakably and disgracefully mean to him in the wintry gloom of the gaslights. She halted before a tenement that seemed even more odious than its neighbours. Was it possible that she should exist in such a quarter? The idea sickened him.

'Which floor?' he questioned.

'Oh,' she laughed, 'the top, the fifth. Good-night, Mr. Hugo.'

He pictured the mean and frowsy room, and shuddered. Yet what could he do? What right had he to interfere, to criticise, to ameliorate?

'Good-night,' she repeated, and in a moment she had opened the door with a latchkey and disappeared. He stood staring at the door. He had by no means finished saying all that he meant to say to her. He must talk to her further. He must show her that he could not be dismissed in that summary fashion. He mounted the two dirty steps, and rang the bell in a determined manner. He heard it tinkle distantly.

She was divine, adorable, marvellous, and far beyond the deserts of any man; but she had not shaken hands with him, and she had treated him as she might have treated one of the shopwalkers. Moreover, the question of to-morrow had to be decided.

There was no answer to the bell, and he rang again, with an increase of energy.

Then he perceived through the fanlight an illumination in the hall. The door opened cautiously, as such doors always do open, and a middle-aged man in a dressing-gown stood before him. In the background he descried a small table with a candle on it, and the foul, polished walls of the narrow lobby—a representative London lodging-house.

'I want to see Mrs. Tudor,' said Hugo.

'Well, she ain't in at the moment,' replied the man.

'Excuse me,' Hugo corrected him, 'I saw her enter a minute ago with her latchkey.'

'No, you didn't,' the man persisted. 'I'm the landlord of this house, and I've been in my room at the back, and nobody's come in this last half-hour, for I can see the 'all and the stairs as I sits in my chair.'

'Wait a moment,' said Hugo; and he retreated to the kerb, in the expectation of being able to descry Camilla's light in the fifth story.

'Oh, you can look,' the landlord observed loftily, divining his intention; 'I warrant there's no light there.'

And there was not.

'Perhaps you'll call again,' said the landlord suavely.

'I suppose you haven't got a room to let?' Hugo demanded, fumbling about in his brain for a plan to meet this swift crisis.

'I can't tell you till my wife comes home.'

'And when will that be?'

'That'll be to-morrow.'

The door was banged to. Hugo rang again, wrathfully, but the door remained obstinate.

CHAPTER XXV

CHLOROFORM

'Come in,' said Simon grandly, in response to a knock.

He was seated in his master's chair in the dome, which was lit as though for a fête. The clock showed the hour of nine.

Albert entered.

'Oh, it's you, is it?' exclaimed Albert. 'Where's the governor?'

'I don't know where he is. He was in his office at something to seven, having an interview with Mrs. Tudor. Since then—'

Simon raised his eyebrows, and Albert expressed a similar sentiment by means of a whistle.

'Then, you've been telephoning on your own for me to come up?'

'Yes.'

'It's like your cheek!' Albert complained, calmly perching himself on the top of the grand piano.

'Perhaps it will be. I regret to tear you from your fireside, Alb, but I wish to consult you on a matter affecting the governor.'

'Go ahead, then,' said Albert. 'There's been enough talk about the governor to-day downstairs, I should hope.'

'You mean in reference to Mrs. Tudor's reappearance?'

'Yes.' Albert imitated Simon's carefully enunciated periods. 'I do mean in reference to Mrs. Tudor's reappearance. By the way, what the deuce are you burning all these lights for?'

'I was examining this photograph,' said Simon, handing to his brother a rather large unmounted silver-print photograph which had lain on his knees.

'What of it?' Albert asked, glancing at it. 'Medical and Pharmaceutical Department, isn't it? Not bad.'

'We're having a new series of full-plate photographs done for the next edition of the General Catalogue,' said Simon, 'and this is one of them. It contains forty-five figures. It was taken yesterday morning by that Curgenven flashlight process that we're running. Look at it. Don't you see anything?'

'Nothing special,' Albert admitted.

Simon rose and came towards the piano.

'Let me show you,' he said superiorly. 'You see the cash-desk to the left. There's a lady just leaving the cash-desk. And just behind her there's an oldish man. You can't see all of his face because of her hat. He's holding his bill in his hand—you can see the corner of it—and he's got some sort of a parcel under his arm. See?'

'Yes, Mr. Lecoq.'

'Well, doesn't he remind you of somebody?'

'He's rather like old Ravengar, perhaps,' said Albert dubiously.

'You've hit it!' Simon almost shouted. 'It is Ravengar.'

'This man's got no beard.'

'That comes well from a detective, that does!' said Simon scornfully. 'It needn't have cost him more than threepence to have his beard shaved off, need it?'

'And seeing that this photograph was taken yesterday morning, and Ravengar fell off a steamer into the Channel more than a week ago!'

'But did he fall off a steamer more than a week ago?'

'He was noticed on board the steamer before she started, and he wasn't on board when she arrived.'

'Couldn't he have walked on to the steamer with his luggage, and then walked off again and let her start without him?'

'But why?'

'Suppose he wanted to pretend to be dead?'

'Why should he want to pretend to be dead?' Albert defended his position.

Simon, entirely forgetful of that dignity which usually he was at such pains to preserve, sprang on to the piano alongside Albert.

'I'll tell you another thing,' said he. 'When I came in with the governor's tea this morning he was just dozing and half-dreaming like—he'd had a very bad night—and I heard him say, "So they think you are at the bottom of the Channel, Louis? I wish you were!" What do you think of that, my son?'

'Then the governor must know Ravengar didn't commit suicide in the Channel? The governor never said a word to me!'

'You don't imagine the governor tells you everything, do you?' said Simon cruelly.

'Have you shown him the photo?' Albert asked.

'No,' said Simon, with a certain bluntness.

'Why not?'

'Well, for one thing, I've had no chance, and for another I wanted to find out something more first. I'd just like the governor to see that I'm not an absolute idiot.... Though I should have thought he might have found that out before now.'

'He doesn't think you're an absolute idiot,' said Albert.

'He acts as if he did,' said Simon. The Paris trip still rankled.

A pause followed.

'Another thing,' Albert recommenced. 'Even supposing Ravengar's alive, it's not very likely he'd venture here, of all places.'

'Why not?' Simon argued. 'Scarcely anybody knows Ravengar by sight. He's famous for keeping himself to himself. He's one of the least known celebrities in London. He'd be safe from recognition almost anywhere. Moreover, supposing he wanted to buy something peculiar?'

'He might,' Albert admitted. 'But don't forget this is all theory. I suppose you've been making your own inquiries in the Medical Department?'

'Yes,' said Simon rather apologetically. 'But I couldn't find anyone among the staff who remembers serving such a man, or even seeing him. He may have had an accomplice, you know, on the staff. What makes it more awkward is that there were two photographs taken, one about eleven, and another about half-past, and the photographer got the plates mixed up, and doesn't know whether this one is the first or the second. You see, the clock doesn't show in the picture; otherwise, we might have pieced things together.'

'Pity!' Albert murmured.

'However,' said Simon, with an obvious intention to be dramatic, 'I thought of Lecoq, and I hit on something. You see the lady just leaving the cash-desk with her receipt? Can you read the number of her receipt?'

Albert peered.

'No, I can't,' he said.

'Neither could I,' Simon agreed. 'But I've had that part of the photograph enlarged to-night.'

'The deuce you have!' Albert opened his eyes.

'Yes, the deuce I have! And here it is.'

Simon took a photographic print from his pocket, showing the lady's hand and part of the receipt, very blurred and faint, with some hieroglyphic figures mistily appearing.

'Looks like 6,706,' said Albert.

'It's either 6,706 or 6,766,' Simon concurred. 'Now, Ravengar's receipt must be numbered next to hers. Consequently, if we go and look at the counterfoils and duplicates—'

'Yes,' said Albert, thoughtfully sliding down from the piano.

'We may be able to find out something very interesting,' Simon finished, descending also.

'Now?'

'Now. That's what I wanted you for. You've got your pass-keys and everything, haven't you?'

'Yes.'

'Then run down and search.'

'Aren't you coming too?'

'I was only thinking, suppose the governor came back and wanted me?'

Albert gazed contemptuously at this exhibition of timidity—the cowardice of a born valet, he deemed it.

'Oh, of course,' he exclaimed, 'if you—'

'I'll come,' said Simon boldly. 'If he wants me he must wait, that's all.'

They descended together in Hugo's private lift, direct from the dome; the Medical and Pharmaceutical Department was on the ground-floor. Simon acted as lift-man, and slammed the grill when they emerged.

'Just open that again, Si,' Albert requested him.

'Why? What's up?'

'Just open it.'

Albert was sniffing about like a dog that is trying to decide whether there is not something extremely attractive in the immediate neighbourhood. He re-entered the lift, and nosed it curiously.

Suddenly he bent down and peered under the cushioned seat of the lift, and drew forth an object that resembled in shape a canister of disinfectant powder.

'Conf—!' he exclaimed, dropping it sharply. 'It's hot. What in the name of—'

He kicked the object out of the lift on to the tessellated floor of a passage which led to the Fish and Game Department.

'I bet you I can hold it,' said Simon boastfully.

And, at the expense of his fingers, he picked it up, and successfully carried it into the Fish and Game Department, where a solitary light (which burnt night and day) threw a dim radiance over vast surfaces of white marble dominated by silver taps. The fish and game were below in the refrigerators. Simon let the cylinder fall on to a slab; Albert turned a tap, and immediately the cylinder was surrounded by clouds of steam. The phenomenon was like some alchemical and mysterious operation. And the steam, as it rose and spread abroad in the immense, pale interior, might have been the fumes of a fatal philtre distilled by a mediæval sorcerer.

'I hope it won't blow up!' Simon ejaculated.

'Not it!' said Albert. 'Let's have a look at it now.'

Albert had a mechanical bent, and, with the aid of a tool, he soon discovered that the cylinder was divided into two parts. In the lower part was burning charcoal. In the upper, carefully closed, was paraffin. The division between the two compartments consisted of some sort of soldering lead, which the heat of the charcoal had gradually been melting.

'So when this stuff had melted,' he explained to Simon, 'the paraffin would run into the charcoal, and there would be a magnificent flare-up.'

They looked at one another, amazed, astounded, speechless.

And each knew that on the tip of the other's tongue, unuttered, was the word 'Ravengar.'

'But why was it put in the lift?' asked Simon.

'Because,' said Albert promptly, 'a lift-well is the finest possible place for a fire. There's a natural draught, and a free chance for every floor. Poof! And a flame's up nine stories in no time. And a really good mahogany lift would burn gorgeously, and give everything a good start.'

'There are fifteen lifts in this place,' Simon muttered.

'I know,' said Albert.

He approached a little glass square in the wall, broke it, pulled a knob, and looked at his watch.

'We'll test the Fire Brigade Department,' he remarked; and then, as he heard a man running down the adjacent corridor, 'Seven seconds. Not bad.'

In another seven minutes nine cylinders, which had been found in nine different lifts, were sizzling beside Albert's original discovery. The other five lifts appeared to have been omitted from this colossal scheme for providing London with a pyrotechnic display such as London had probably never had since the year 1666. The night fire staff, which consisted of some fifty men, had laid hose on to every hydrant, and were taking instructions from their chief for the incessant patrol of the galleries.

'See here,' said Albert, 'we'd better go on with what we started of now.'

'Had we?' Simon questioned somewhat dubiously.

'Of course,' said Albert. 'If that is Ravengar in the photo, and if we can find out anything to-night, and if Ravengar's in this business'—he jerked his elbow towards the cylinders—'we shall be so much to the good. Besides, it won't take us a minute.'

So they went forward, through twilit chambers and passages filled with sheeted objects, past miles of counters inhabited by thousands of chairs, through doors whose openings resounded strangely in the vast nocturnal silence of Hugo's, till they came to the Medical and Pharmaceutical Department. And the Medical and Pharmaceutical Department, in its night-garb, and illuminated by a single jet at either end of it, seemed to take on a kind of ghostly and scented elegance; it seemed to be a lunar palace of bizarre perfumes and crystal magics.

The two young men halted, and listened, and they could catch the distant footfall of the patrols echoing in some far-off corridor. That reassured them. They ceased to fancy the smell of burning and to be victimized by the illusion that a little tongue of flame darted out behind them.

Albert gained access to the accountant's cupboard, and pulled out a number of books, over which they pored side by side.

'Here you are!' exclaimed Simon presently. 'Receipts. January 9.'

And Albert read: 'No. 6,766, Mrs. Poidevin, 37, Prince's Gate; vinolia. No. 6,767, Dr. Woolrich, 23, Horseferry Road; chloroform! Can't make out the quantity, but it must be a lot, I should think; the price is eighteen and ninepence.'

'Dr. Woolrich, 23, Horseferry Road?' Simon repeated mechanically. 'Chloroform?'

'That's it,' said Albert. 'You may bet your boots. Let's look him up in the Medical Directory, if they've got one here. Yes, they're sure to have one.'

But there was no Dr. Woolrich in the Medical Directory.

Once more the brothers stared at each other. Was or was not Ravengar alive? Were they or were they not on his track?

'Listen, Si,' said Albert. 'I'll drive right down to 23, Horseferry Road, and have a look round. Eh? What do you say?'

'I think I'll come, too,' Simon replied.

In six minutes Albert pulled up the hansom at the end of the street, and they walked slowly towards No. 23, but on the opposite side of the road.

'That's it,' said Simon, pointing. 'What are you going to do now? Inquire there?'

At the same moment a window opened behind them, in the house immediately facing No. 23; they both heard a hissing sound, evidently designed to attract their attention, and they both turned their heads.

From a first-story window Hugo was gesticulating at them.

CHAPTER XXVI

SECOND TRIUMPH OF SIMON

'Come up at once,' Hugo whispered. 'Door opposite top of stairs.'

And he threw down on to the pavement a latchkey.

'What do you think of yourself now, Si?' Albert asked his brother, as they entered the house. 'You've let yourself in for something at last.'

They found Hugo in an ordinary bedsitting-room. He was wearing his hat and his overcoat, and staring out of the open window. It was a cold night, but he did not seem to feel the icy draught which blew into the apartment. The whole of his attention appeared to be concentrated on No. 23. He did not at first even turn to look at the brothers when they came in. They explained themselves.

'I will tell you why I am here, and what has occurred to me,' said Hugo, playing, perhaps rather nervously, with the knife and cheese-plate which still lay on the small table by the window. 'Then we can decide what to do. I've hired this room.'

No doubt existed in his mind that Simon had happened upon the track of the veritable living Ravengar. It could not be a coincidence that a man so strongly resembling Ravengar, a man posing as a doctor, and buying nearly a sovereign's worth of chloroform, should be occupying rooms in the same house as Camilla. The tremendous revelation of Ravengar's genius for stratagem and intrigue afforded by the recital of the two brothers came upon Hugo with a dazing shock. This man, whom he knew from Camilla's own story to be curiously deficient in ordinary human sentiments, had arranged a sham suicide for the benefit of the general public. He had let Hugo into the secret of that deception, but only to cheat him with another deception, and a more monstrous one. The brain that could conceive the fiction of suicide in the vault—a fiction which, while lulling Hugo into a false security as regards Camilla's safety, at the same time poisoned his happiness—such a brain might be capable of unimagined horrors. Sane or mad, the mere existence of that brain was a menace before which Hugo trembled. He realized that Ravengar had been consummately acting during the latter part of their interview on the first day of the sale, and again consummately acting when he spoke to Hugo on the telephone. Ravengar had, beyond doubt, deliberately set himself to lure Camilla back to England, and he had succeeded. Beyond doubt, all her movements had been spied and marked, and Ravengar had been in a position to complete his arrangements—whatever his arrangements were—at leisure and with absolute freedom. She had taken a room in Horseferry Road, and he had followed.... What was the sequel to be?

That she was in his power at that moment Hugo could not question.

And the chloroform?

At that moment Ravengar had meant that the Hugo building should have been a funeral pyre—a spectacle to petrify the Metropolis. And it seemed to Hugo that if Ravengar was mad, as he must be, he could only have designed the spectacle as something final, as at once a last revenge and an accompaniment to the supreme sacrifice of Camilla.

'We must get into that house immediately,' said Hugo, when he had finished his own narrative. 'The question is how?'

'I've got a card of Inspector Wilbraham's, of the Yard, in my pocket,' Albert suggested. 'We might use that, and make out that this purchase of chloroform under a false name had got to be explained to the Yard instantly.'

Albert had recently become rather intimate with Scotland Yard. Inspector Wilbraham had even called on him in reference to Bentley's death and the disappearance of Brown; and Albert was duly proud.

'We will try that,' said Hugo. 'Have you any handcuffs?'

'No, sir.'

'Go and obtain a couple of pairs. You can be back in twenty minutes. Bring also my revolver.'

Hugo and Simon were left alone. Hugo spoke no word.

'I'll put the room to rights, sir,' said Simon, after a pause. He could bear the inaction no longer.

Hugo nodded absently, and Simon collected the ruins of the vile repast which his master had consumed, and put them outside on a tray on the landing.

'There's a light now in the first story!' exclaimed Hugo. 'I hope that boy won't be long.'

And then Albert arrived with the revolver and the handcuffs. He had been supernaturally quick.

They descended and crossed the road.

'You understand,' Hugo instructed them. 'Let us have no mistake about getting in. Immediately the door is opened, in we all go. We can talk inside.'

'Supposing Albert and me went down to the area-door,' Simon ventured, 'instead of the front-door. We might get in easier that way. It's always easier to deal with servant-girls and persons of that sort in kitchens. Then we could come upstairs and let you in at the front-door. Three detectives seem rather a lot to be entering all at once. And, besides, you don't look like a detective, sir.'

'What do I look like?' Hugo asked coldly.

'You look too much like a gentleman, sir. It's the hat, sir,' he added.

Simon had certainly surpassed himself that day. He had begun by surpassing himself at early morning, and he had kept it up. Probably never before in his life had he been so loquacious and so happy in his loquacity.

'That's not a bad scheme, Simon,' said Hugo. 'Try it.'

The brothers went down the area-steps while Hugo remained at the gate. A light burned steadily in the first-floor window. And then another and a fainter light flickered in the hall, and after a few seconds the front-door opened. Hugo literally jumped into the house, and, safely within, he banged the door.

'Now,' he said.

A middle-aged woman, holding a candle, stood by Simon and Albert in the hall.

'Are you the servant?' Hugo demanded.

'No, sir; I'm the landlady. And I'd like to know—'

'Your husband told me you were away and wouldn't return till to-morrow.'

'Seeing as how my husband's been dead these thirteen years—'

'We're in, sir. We'd better search the house to start with,' said Albert. 'There's three of us. The man that opened the door to you must have been a wrong un, one of *his*.'

'Never have I had the police in my house before,' wailed the landlady of No. 23, Horseferry Road, while the candle dropped tallow tears on the oilcloth. 'And all I can say is I thank the blessed Lord it's dark, and you aren't in uniform. Doctor Woolrich's rooms are on the first floor, and you can go up and see for yourself, if you like. And how should I know he wasn't a real doctor?'

As the landlady spoke, sounds of footsteps made themselves heard overhead, and a door closed.

'Give me that candle, my good woman,' said Hugo, hastily snatching it from her.

The three men ran upstairs, leaving the hall to darkness and the landlady.

Whether Hugo dropped the candle in his excitement, or whether it was knocked out of his hand by means of a stick through the rails of the landing-banister as he ascended, will never be accurately known. He himself is not sure. The important fact is that the candle fell, and the trio stumbled up the last few stairs with nothing to guide them but a chink of light through a half-closed door. This door led to the rooms of Dr. Woolrich, and the rooms of Dr. Woolrich were well lighted with gas. But they were empty. There was a sitting-room and a bedroom, and on the round table in the centre of the sitting-room was a copy of the most modern edition of Quain's 'Dictionary of Medicine,' edited by Murray, Harold, and Bosanquet, bound in half-morocco; the volume was open at the article 'Anæsthetics,' and Hugo will always remember that the page was sixty-two. No sooner were the rooms found to be empty than Hugo rushed back to the landing, followed by Simon. The landing, however, even with the sitting-room door thrown wide and the light streaming across the landing and down the stairs, showed no sign of life.

Then Albert, who had remained within the suite, called out:

'There must be a dressing-room off this bedroom, and it's locked.'

'Simon,' said Hugo, 'go to the front window and keep watch.'

And Hugo ran into the bedroom to Albert.

Decidedly there was a door in the bedroom which had the appearance of leading into a further room, but the door would not budge. The pair glanced about. No evidence of recent human habitation was visible either in the sitting-room or in the bedroom, save only the dictionary, and Albert commented on this.

'We must force that door,' Hugo decided, 'and be ready to look after yourself when it gives way.'

As he spoke he could see, in the tail of his eye, Simon opening the front window and then looking out into the street.

'One—two—charge!' cried Hugo; and he and Albert flung themselves valiantly against the door.

They made no impression upon it at all.

Breathless and shaken, they looked at each other.

'Suppose I fire into the lock?' said Hugo.

'We might try a key first,' Albert answered.

He took the key from the door between the bedroom and the sitting-room, and applied it to the lock of the obstinate portal. The obstinate portal opened at once.

'Empty!' ejaculated Albert, putting his nose into a small dressing-room.

With a gesture of disgust Hugo turned away. In the same instant Simon withdrew his head into the sitting-room.

'I've seen him,' Simon whispered in hoarse excitement. 'He just popped out of the kitchen and came half-way up the area steps. Then he ran back. He saw me looking at him.'

'Ravengar?'

Simon nodded. This was the hour of Simon's triumph, the proof that he had not been mistaken in the theory which he had raised on the foundation of the photograph.

'Come along,' said Hugo grimly, preparing to rush downstairs.

But a singular thing had occurred. While Simon had been staring out of the front window, and Hugo and Albert engaged in forcing a door which led to emptiness, the door of the sitting-room, the sole means of egress from the first-floor suite, had been shut and locked on the outside.

In vain Hugo assailed it with boot and shoulder; in vain Albert assisted him.

'Keep your eye on the street, you fool!' said Albert to Simon, when the latter offered to join the siege of the door.

Hugo and Albert multiplied their efforts.

'There's a cab driven up,' Simon informed them from the window. 'A man's got out. Now he's gone down the area steps. They're carrying something up, something big. Oh! look here, I must help you.'

And Simon ran to the door. Before the triple assault it fell at last, and the three tumbled pell-mell downstairs into the hall. The front-door was open.

A cab was just driving away. It drove rapidly, very rapidly.

'After it!' Hugo commanded.

The hunt was up.

Two minutes afterwards another cab drove up to the door.

Ravengar and another man emerged from the area holding between them the form of a woman. They got leisurely into the cab with the woman and departed.

CHAPTER XXVII

THE CEMETERY

Both Simon and Albert easily outran Hugo, and, fast as the first cab was travelling, they had gained on it by the time it turned into Victoria Street. And at the turning an incident happened. The driver, though hurried, was apparently to a certain extent careful and cautious, but he did not altogether avoid contact with a policeman at the corner. The policeman was obliged to step sharply out of the way of the cab, and even then the sleeve of his immaculate tunic was soiled by contact with the hind-wheel of the vehicle. Now, the driver might have scraped an ordinary person with impunity, and passed on unchallenged; he might even have soiled the sleeve of a veteran policeman and got nothing worse than a sharp word of censure and a fragment of good advice. But this particular policeman was quite a new policeman, whose dignity was as delicate and easily smirched as his beautiful shining tunic. And the result was that the cabby had to stop, give his number, and listen to a lecture.

Simon and Albert formed part of the audience for the lecture. It did not, however, interest them, for they had instantly perceived that the cab was empty.

Then, as the lecturer was growing eloquent, Hugo arrived, and was informed of the emptiness of the vehicle.

'It was just a trick,' Simon exclaimed; 'a trick to get us out of the house.'

'We must go back,' said Hugo, breathless.

At this moment the second cab appeared, was delayed a moment by the multitude listening to the lecture, and passed westwards into Victoria Street.

'They're in that!' cried Simon.

'Are you sure?' Hugo questioned.

'Of course I'm sure,' said Simon, who in the excitement of the trail had ceased to be a valet.

To jump into a hansom and order the driver to keep the four-wheeler in sight ought to have been the work of a few seconds, but it occurred, as invariably occurs when a hansom is urgently needed, that no hansom was available. The four-wheeler was receding at a moderate rate in the direction of the Grosvenor Hotel.

'Run after it!' said Hugo. 'I'll get a cab in the station-yard and follow.'

The quarry vanished round a corner just as they tumbled into the hansom on the top of Hugo, but it was never out of observation for more than a quarter of a minute. Through divers strange streets it came at length into Fulham Road at Elm Place, and thenceforward, at a higher rate of speed, it kept to the main thoroughfare. The procession passed the workhouse and the Redcliffe Arms. Between Edith Grove and Stamford Bridge the roadway was up for fundamental repairs, and omnibuses were being diverted down Edith Grove to King's Road. A policeman at the corner spoke to the driver of the four-wheeler, gave a sign of assent, and the four-wheeler went straight onwards into a medley of wood-blocks, which was all that was left of Fulham Road. The hansom followed intrepidly, and then its three occupants were conscious of a sudden halt.

'Bobby wants to know where you're going to,' said the driver, opening the trap.

There was a slight hesitation, and the policeman's voice could be heard:

'Come out of it!'

'We're following that four-wheeler,' Hugo was about to say, but he perceived the absurdity of saying such a thing in cold blood to a policeman.

All three descended. The cabman had to be paid. There was a difficulty about finding change—one of those silly and ridiculous difficulties that so frequently supervene in crises otherwise grave; in short, a succession of trifling delays, each of which might easily have been obviated by perfect forethought, or by perfect accord between the three men.

When next they came to close quarters with the four-wheeler it was leisurely driving away empty from a small semi-detached house which was separated from the road by a tiny garden. They ran into the garden. The one thing that flourished in it was a 'To Let' notice. The front-door, shaded by unpruned trees, was shut, and there were cobwebs on the handle, as Hugo plainly saw when he struck a match. They hastened round to the back of the house, where was a larger garden. A French window gave access to the house. This French window yielded at once to a firm push. The three men searched the ground-floor and found nothing. They then ascended the stairs and equally found nothing. The house must have been empty for many months. From the first-floor window at the back Hugo gazed out, baffled. Far off he could see lights of houses, but the foreground was all darkness and mystery.

'What lies between us and those lights?' he asked.

'It must be Brompton Cemetery, sir,' said Albert. 'The garden gives on the cemetery, I expect.'

As if suddenly possessed by a demon, Hugo flew out of the room, down the stairs, into the garden. At the extremity of the garden was a brick wall, and against the wall were two extremely convenient barrels; they might have been placed there specially for the occasion. In an instant he was in the cemetery.

The remainder of the adventure survives in Hugo's memory like a sort of night-picture in which all the minor details of life are lost in large, vague glooms, and only the central figures of the composition emerge clearly, in a sharp and striking brilliance, against the mysterious background.

He knew himself in the cemetery, and immediately, by a tremendous effort of the brain, he had arranged his knowledge of the place and decided exactly where he was. Instinctively he ran by side-alleys till he came to the broad central way which cuts this vast field of the dead north and south. He hurried northwards, and when he had gone about a hundred and fifty yards he turned to the left, and then went north again.

'It's here,' he muttered.

He was in the middle of that strange and sinister city within a city, that flat expanse of silence, decay, and putrefaction which is surrounded on every side by the pulsating arteries of London. The living visit the dead during the day, but at night the dead are left to themselves, and the very flowers which embroider their dissolution close up and forget them. Round about him everywhere trees and shrubs moved restlessly and plaintively in the night breeze; the angular grave-stones raised their kindly lies in the darkness. A few stars flickered in the sky; no moon. And miles off, so it seemed, north, south, east, and west, the yellow lights of human habitations, the lights of warm rooms where living people were so engaged in the business of being alive that they actually forgot death—these lights winked to each other across the waste and desolation of a hundred thousand tombs.

With the certainty of a blind man, the assurance of a seer who has divined what the future holds, he approached the vault. He was aware that the little gate in the railing would be open. It was. He was aware that the iron door in the side of the vault would be unlocked. It was. He pushed it and entered. All difficulties and hindrances had been removed. No odour of death greeted his nostrils, unless the strong smell of chloroform can be called the odour of death. He struck a match. The first thing he saw was a candle and a screwdriver, and then the match blew out. The door of the vault was ajar, and he would not close it. He dared not. He struck another match and put it to the candle, and the vault was full of jumping shadows. And he looked and looked again. Yes, down in that corner she lay, motionless, lifeless, done with for ever and ever. Only her face was visible. The rest of her seemed to be covered with a man's overcoat, flung hastily down. He stared, enchanted by the horror. What was that white stuff round her head? Part of it seemed to be torn, and a strip fluttered across her closed eyelids. He went nearer. He touched—cold! Could she be so soon cold? And then the truth swept over him, and almost swept his senses away, that this image in the corner was not she, but merely that waxen thing made by the sculptor in Paris, that counterfeit which had deceived him in the drawing-room of the flat.

Then where was she? And why was not this counterfeit in its coffin, in which it had been buried with all the rites of the Church? The coffin? Yes, the coffin was there at his feet, with its brass plate, which had rusted at the corners; and below it, in some undefined depth, was another coffin, the sarcophagus of Tudor himself. He stooped and shifted the candle. On Camilla's coffin were a number of screws, rolled about in various directions; only one screw was in its place. He seized the screwdriver—and in that moment a tiny part of his intelligence found leisure to decide that this screwdriver was slightly longer than the one he had used aforetime for a similar purpose—and he unscrewed the solitary screw and raised the lid of the coffin, letting all the screws roll off it with a great rattle.... An overwhelming rush of chloroform vapour escaped.... She lay within, dressed in her black dress, and her dress had been crammed into the coffin hastily, madly, and was thrust down in thick, disorderly folds about her feet, and her hair half covered her face. And her face was slightly flushed, and her eyelids quivered, and the cheeks were warm. He put his hands under her armpits and wrenched her out and carried her from the vault. And then he sank to the ground sobbing.

What caused him to sob? If any man dared now to ask him, and if he dared to answer, he might reply that it was not grief nor joy, nor the reaction from an intolerable strain, but simply the idea of the terrific and heart-breaking cruelty of Ravengar which had dragged from him a sob.

The path followed by the madman's brain was easy to pursue once the clue found. He had been cheated into the belief that Camilla's body rested in that coffin, and when he had discovered that it did not rest there he had determined that the mistake should be rectified, the false made true. That had seemed to him logical and just. She was supposed to be in the coffin; she should really be in the coffin; she should be forced and jammed into it. And his lunatic and inhuman fancy had added even to that conception. She should be drugged and carried to the vault, and drugged again, and then immured, unconscious, but alive; and if by chance she awoke from the chloroform sleep after he had finished screwing in the screws, so much the better! So it was that his mind had worked. And the scheme had been executed with that courage, that calmness, that audacity, that minute attention to detail, of which only madmen at their maddest appear to be capable. Beyond any question the scheme would have succeeded had not Hugo, the moment Albert Shawn uttered the word 'cemetery,' perceived the general trend of it in a single wondrous flash of intuition. He had guessed it, and even while afraid to believe that he was right, had known absolutely and convincingly that he was right.

Camilla murmured some phrase, and gave a sigh as she lay on the gravelled path.

She had recovered from the fatal torpor in the cool night air. He said nothing, because he felt that he could do nothing else. Albert and Simon were certainly looking for him in the maze of the cemetery; they would find him soon. It did not seem to him extraordinary that he had left them in that sudden, swift fashion without a word.

Then he heard, or thought he heard, a noise in the vault, and, summoning all his strength of will, he descended the steps again and glanced within. Ravengar was there. Had he been there all the time, hidden behind the door? Or had he fled and stealthily returned? Only Ravengar could say. He had taken up the image from the corner and was replacing it in the coffin. It was as if he had bowed his obstinate purpose to some higher power which was inscrutable to him. Children and madmen can practise this singular and surprising fatalism. Disturbed, he raised his head and caught sight of Hugo. They gazed at one another by the flickering candle.

'Where's the man who helped you?' Hugo demanded faintly.

He had not much heart, much force, much firmness left. Ravengar's eyes, at once empty and significant, blank and yet formidable, startled him. He had the revolver and the handcuffs in his pocket, but he could not have used them. Ravengar's eyes, so fiendish and so ineffably sad, melted his spine. Ravengar stepped forward and Hugo stepped back.

'Let me pass,' said Ravengar, in the tone of one who has suffered much and does not mean to suffer much more.

And Hugo let him pass, inexplicably, weakly; and at the end of a narrow path he merged into the vague, general darkness. And then Hugo heard the sound of a struggle, and the voices of Simon and Albert—young and boisterous and earthly and sane. And then scampering footfalls which died away in the uttermost parts of the cemetery.

And Camilla sat up, rubbing her eyes.

'It's all right,' he soothed her.

CHAPTER XXVIII

BEAUTY

'Hum! he's going to marry her,' Simon had said, and Albert had said, and Lily had said. 'I knew it all along.' When, at the end of six months, Hugo went away, much furnishing of rooms near the Dome took place by his orders during his absence.

Yet here was Hugo back at the end of the fortnight, radiant certainly, but alone.

'There was one little matter I forgot,' Hugo began, rather timidly, as Simon thought, when assured that everything was in order.

'Yes, sir?' said Simon.

'I want you to be good enough to give up your room.'

'My room, sir?'

'To oblige a lady.'

'A lady, sir?'

'I should say a lady's lady.'

Simon paused. He was wounded, but he would not show it.

'With pleasure, sir.'

'To-night,' Hugo proceeded, 'you can occupy my bed in the dome;' and he pointed to the spot where, during the day, the bed lay ingeniously hidden in a recess of the wall. 'I shall no longer need it. To-morrow we can make some more permanent arrangement for you.'

'Yes, sir.'

'Also,' Hugo continued, 'I would like you to go along to the offices of the *Morning Post* for me some time to-night before ten o'clock and take this. There will be a guinea to pay.' Hugo handed him a slip of paper.

'Yes, sir.'

'Read it,' said Hugo.

And Simon read: '"A marriage has been arranged, and"—and—has taken place, sir?'

'Precisely.'

'Precisely, sir. "Has taken place at Hythe between Mr. Owen Hugo, of Sloane Street, London, and Mrs. Camilla Tudor, widow of the late Mr. Francis Tudor."'

'You are the first to know, Simon.'

Simon bowed.

'May I respectfully venture to wish you every happiness, sir?' Simon pronounced at his most formal.

'No, you may not,' said Hugo. 'But you may shake hands with me.'

And he respectfully ventured to explain to Simon how, in the case of a man like himself, with three thousand five hundred tongues ever ready to wag about him, absolute secrecy had been the only policy.

'Telephone down to the refreshment department for Tortoni to come up to me instantly. I must order a dinner for two. My wife and her maid will be here in half an hour. I shall not want you—at any rate, before ten-thirty or so.'

'Yes, sir. And the maid?'

'What about the maid?'

'You said you would order dinner for two, sir.'

'Look here, Simon,' said Hugo. 'If you will take the maid down to dine in the Central Restaurant and keep her there—take her with you for a drive to the *Morning Post*—I shall regard it as a favour. Catch!' And he threw to Simon the gold token, which made Simon master of all the good things in the entire building. 'Make use of that.'

Simon felt a little nervous at the prospect. He had not seen the maid. However, he hoped for the best, and assured Hugo of his delight.

'I forgot to inform you, sir,' he turned back to tell Hugo as he was leaving the room, 'Doctor Darcy called again to-day. He has called several times the last few days. He said he might look in again to-night.'

The bridegroom started.

'If he should,' Hugo ordered, 'don't say I'm in till you've warned me.'

'Yes, sir.'

Three hours later the bride and bridegroom were finishing one of the distinguished Tortoni's most elaborate dinners. Tortoni had protested that it was destructive of the elementary principles of art to order a dinner for eight-thirty at seven o'clock. However, he had not completely failed. The waiters had departed, and Camilla, in dazzling ivory-white, was pouring out coffee. Hugo was cutting a cigar. They did not speak; they felt. They were at the end of the brief honeymoon, and the day was at an end. The last remnants of twilight had vanished, and through the eastern windows of the dome the moon was rising. Neither the hour nor the occasion made for talkativeness. Life lay before Hugo and Camilla. Both were honestly convinced that they had not lived till that hour—that hour whence dated the commencement of their regular united existence. They looked at each other, satisfied, admiring, happy, expecting glorious things from Fate.

There was a discreet alarm at the door. Simon came in. It would have been a gross solecism to knock, but Simon performed the equivalent. He paused, struck when he beheld Camilla, as well he might; for Camilla was such a vision as is not often vouchsafed to the Simons of this world. She was peerless that evening. And she smiled charmingly on him, and asked after his health.

'Your coffee, dearest,' she murmured to Hugo.

It occurred to Simon that the dome would never be the same again. This miraculous and amazing creature was going to be always there, to form part of his daily life, to swish her wonderful skirts in and out of the rooms, to—to—He did not know whether to be glad or sorry. He knew only that he was perturbed, thrown off his balance, so much so that he forgot to explain his invasion.

'Well, Simon,' said Hugo, 'had your dinner and been to the *Morning Post* office?'

'Yes, sir.'

'Alone?'

Simon blushed.

'No, sir.'

'Good.'

'Doctor Darcy is here, sir. Are you at home?'

Hugo had utterly forgotten about Doctor Darcy. He glanced at his wife interrogatively, but Camilla looked at the moon through the window.

'Show Doctor Darcy in in five minutes,' said Hugo.

'Poor old Darcy!' exclaimed Camilla when they were alone. 'Does he know?'

'Know what? That we are married? No. I wrote to him nearly six months ago to tell him that you were safe and all that, and he acknowledged the letter on a postcard. Afterwards I sent him that trifle of money that you owed him, and he sent a stamped receipt.'

'He always hides his feelings,' said Camilla. 'This will be a blow for him!'

'How?'

'Didn't he tell you he was most violently in love with me in Paris?'

'He did not,' said Hugo. 'Did he tell *you*?'

'No, of course not. He was far too chivalrous for that. It would have seemed like taking advantage of my situation to force me into a marriage.'

'How do you know he was violently in love with you, bright star?' Hugo demanded in that amiably malicious tone which he could never withstand the temptation to employ.

'My precious boy,' replied Camilla, 'how *does* a woman know these things?'

And she came over and kissed Hugo.

'You shall talk to him first,' she said. 'I'll join you later.'

'Did he ever commit sublime follies for you,' Hugo asked, detaining her hand, 'as I did when I shut up the entire place because I thought you looked exhausted one hot morning?'

She bent over him.

'Darcy is incapable of any folly in regard to women,' she said. 'That is one reason why we should never have suited each other, he and I. A fool should always marry a fool. Consider *my* folly when I came back to work in your Department 42 simply because I could not forget your masterful face. Wasn't that also sublime?'

'You never told me—'

'But you guessed.'

'Perhaps.'

She withdrew her hand, and then that delicious swish of skirts which Simon's imagination had foretold thrilled Hugo with delight. He launched a kiss towards her as she vanished.

'We are all to be heartily congratulated,' said Darcy, somewhat astonished when Hugo had put him abreast of the times. 'At one period I suspected that you were going to make a match of it, and then, as I heard nothing, I began to be afraid that she had been unable to banish my humble self from her mind. And, to tell you the truth, the object of this present visit to London was to inform myself, and, if necessary, to—offer her—See?'

Hugo was bound to admit that he saw. Inwardly he laughed to think that he had been seriously disturbed by Darcy's statement in regard to the condition of Camilla's heart.

'Shall we go out to the top of the dome?' he suggested.

They rose.

And at that juncture Camilla reappeared.

The greeting between the Paris friends was commendably calm, but neither seemed to be able to speak freely. And at length Camilla said she would get a cloak and follow them to the belvidere.

The two men climbed to the summit which dominated the City of Pleasure. To the east the famous roof restaurant glittered and jingled under the moon. To the west the Great Wheel was outlined in flame—a symbol of the era. Hugo told Darcy the history of the night in the cemetery, and what preceded, and what came after it, including the strange death of Ravengar in a lunatic asylum, and how everything was explained or explicable—even Mr. Brown, the manager of the Safe Deposit, had run up against justice in Caracas—save and except the identity of Ravengar's accomplice during the last days. He was enlarging upon the inscrutability of that part of the affair, and upon the interest which it lent to the whole episode, when Darcy, who had not been listening, broke in upon his observation with an inapposite remark which obviously sprang from deep feeling.

'She's simply marvellous!' cried Darcy.

'Who?'

'Your wife. Simply marvellous! I had no idea—in Paris—'

'Recollect, you are not in love with her, my friend,' Hugo laughed.

'She must have the best blood in her veins. With that style, that carriage, she surely must be—'

'My dear fellow,' said Hugo, 'beauty has no rank. It bloweth where it listeth. It is the one thing in the world that you can't account for. You've only got to be thankful for it when it blows your way, that's all.'

A white figure appeared in the cavity of the steps leading to the circular gallery.

'What are you talking about?' Camilla inquired.

'Women,' said Hugo.

THE END

Printed in the USA
CPSIA information can be obtained
at www.ICGtesting.com
LVHW080252281024
794972LV00004B/174